What people are saying about

EXILES

"The Left and the Right don't just want your vote; they want your soul. So it's no surprise that, in the absence of an alternate political vision, many Christians are hitching their theological wagons to secular political programs. In *Exiles*, Preston Sprinkle shows that Jesus offers a better way. Only a church of exiles—those who pledge allegiance to Jesus over the empire—can cut across our tired political divisions and become the subversive, loving, self-sacrificial counterculture that God calls us to be. *Exiles* is a must-read for pastors and leaders desperate to win people to a kingdom-centered vision of political identity that's far more compelling and satisfying than the culture war."

Patrick Miller, pastor, author and
co-host of *Truth Over Tribe*

"Allegiance to the American empire and religious devotion to partisan politics has resulted in a deeply compromised church. Instead of offering the beautiful alternative found in the gospel of Jesus Christ, far too many Christians have become zealous combatants in America's corrosive culture wars. It's in this context that *Exiles: The Church in the Shadow of Empire* arrives as a word from elsewhere. With careful attention to the biblical text, Preston Sprinkle calls us to emulate faithful Jewish exiles in Babylon and early Christians in the Roman Empire by living as true citizens of the kingdom of God. This book is just what we need!"

Brian Zahnd, author of *Postcards from Babylon*

"Preston Sprinkle's *Exiles: The Church in the Shadow of Empire* is the most exciting book of biblical theology I have read in a long time. Thoroughly researched, both bold and nuanced, and written in an engaging and understandable style, it should be read by every Christian, leader or lay, who wants the church to understand the biblical call to discipleship in our contemporary social and political contexts."

Michael J. Gorman, Raymond E. Brown
professor of Biblical and Theological Studies,
St. Mary's Seminary & University, Baltimore

"Preston Sprinkle brings a mixture of scriptural exploration and cultural commentary on how the church should live out its faith in an age of empires and extremists and among pundits and powers. He plots a wise course that is neither isolationist nor seeking to be a combatant in an ongoing culture war. People of all stripes of Christian faith will benefit from Sprinkle's diagnosis of the problem and how the church can unhitch itself from the empires of its own day."

Rev. Dr. Michael F. Bird, deputy principal
at Ridley College, Melbourne, Australia

"Sprinkle does what is necessary in Christian political discourse—he brings us back to the Bible. By situating our story in the larger sweep of the biblical narrative, he demonstrates how politics is not a separate sphere for Christians but at the very core of our discipleship to Jesus. This book challenges party loyalists, and while people might disagree with how he describes ordering our allegiances, I hope it will spur on a new generation of faithful witnesses to the King of Kings."

Patrick Schreiner, associate professor of New Testament and Biblical Theology, Midwestern Baptist Theological Seminary; author of *Political Gospel, The Visual Word,* and *The Kingdom of God and the Glory of the Cross*

"In this cultural moment, it is common to want to wrestle well with the question 'How should we as Christians engage meaningfully within the secular and political world?' Preston draws us a map to engage this issue by looking at the biblical narratives of the original biblical exiles, Christ Himself, and the early church. By investigating these examples, *Exiles* provides a great depth and breadth of biblical wisdom that enables us to start doing the good and challenging work of being a prophetic witness in the world today."

Brenna Blain, contemporary theologian and author

NEW YORK TIMES BESTSELLING AUTHOR

PRESTON SPRINKLE

EXILES

THE CHURCH
IN THE SHADOW
OF EMPIRE

DAVID C COOK

transforming lives together

EXILES
Published by David C Cook
4050 Lee Vance Drive
Colorado Springs, CO 80918 U.S.A.

Integrity Music Limited, a Division of David C Cook
Brighton, East Sussex BN1 2RE, England

DAVID C COOK® and related marks are trademarks of David C Cook.

All rights reserved. Except for brief excerpts for review purposes,
no part of this book may be reproduced or used in any form
without written permission from the publisher.

The website addresses recommended throughout this book are offered as a resource
to you. These websites are not intended in any way to be or imply an endorsement
on the part of David C Cook, nor do we vouch for their content.

Unless otherwise noted, all Scripture quotations are taken from the Holy Bible, New International Version®, NIV®. Copyright © 1973, 2011 by Biblica, Inc.™ Used by permission of Zondervan. All rights reserved worldwide. www.zondervan.com. The "NIV" and "New International Version" are trademarks registered in the United States Patent and Trademark Office by Biblica, Inc.™ Scripture quotations marked CSB are taken from the Christian Standard Bible®, Copyright © 2017 by Holman Bible Publishers, and HCSB are taken from the Holman Christian Standard Bible®, Copyright © 1999, 2009 by Holman Bible Publishers. Used by permission. Christian Standard Bible®, CSB®, Holman Christian Standard Bible®, Holman CSB®, and HCSB® are federally registered trademarks of Holman Bible Publishers; ESV are taken from the ESV® Bible (The Holy Bible, English Standard Version®), copyright © 2001 by Crossway, a publishing ministry of Good News Publishers. Used by permission. All rights reserved; NASB are taken from the (NASB®) New American Standard Bible®, Copyright © 1960, 2020 by The Lockman Foundation. Used by permission. All rights reserved. www.lockman.org; NKJV are taken from the New King James Version®. Copyright © 1982 by Thomas Nelson. Used by permission. All rights reserved; NLT are taken from the Holy Bible, New Living Translation, copyright © 1996, 2015 by Tyndale House Foundation. Used by permission of Tyndale House Publishers, Carol Stream, Illinois 60188. All rights reserved; NRSVUE are taken from the New Revised Standard Version, Updated Edition. Copyright © 2021 National Council of Churches of Christ in the United States of America, and RSV are taken from the Revised Standard Version of the Bible, Copyright © 1946, 1971 National Council of the Churches of Christ in the United States of America. Used by permission. All rights reserved worldwide. The author has added italics and bold to Scripture quotations for emphasis.

Library of Congress Control Number 2023945309
ISBN 978-0-8307-8578-0
eISBN 978-0-8307-8579-7

© 2024 Preston Sprinkle

The Team: Michael Covington, Greg Coles, Stephanie Bennett, Judy Gillispie,
Kayla Fenstermaker, James Hershberger, Susan Murdock
Cover Design: James Hershberger
Cover Photo: Getty Images

Printed in the United States of America
First Edition 2024

1 2 3 4 5 6 7 8 9 10

120723

CONTENTS

Chapter 1

THE POLITICS OF CHURCH

Going to church is a politically subversive act. Or at least, it used to be.

Most people who hear the word *church* today think of a church building with a cross hanging on the front wall, Sunday services and sermons, worship bands, sharply dressed families, and cheap coffee served with powdered creamer (or, for the hipster megachurches, a Guatemalan dark roast with oat milk). But a first-century merchant in Corinth would have heard something very different. The original meaning of *church* was profoundly political.

The Greek word translated "church" is *ekklēsia*, and it's used all over the place in the New Testament (114 times, to be exact). Christians didn't invent the word, however. *Ekklēsia* was a well-known political word in the Greek and Roman world long before Christians started using it to describe their communities.[1]

In ancient Greece, the *ekklēsia* was "the regular gathering of male Athenian citizens to listen to, discuss, and vote on decrees that affected every aspect of Athenian life, both public and private."[2] This group would gather thirty to forty times a year and vote on many political issues, "from financial matters to religious ones, from public festivals to war, from treaties with foreign powers to regulations governing ferry boats."[3] The *ekklēsia* of Athens was indeed "the most central and most definitive institution of the Athenian democracy."[4]

In the first-century Roman world, *ekklēsia* retained many of its political connotations from ancient Greece.[5] A civic gathering was called an *ekklēsia*, where certain male citizens would gather and make political and religious decisions.[6] A "preacher" (*kēryx*, also translated "herald") would call an *ekklēsia*; once the group gathered, they would offer prayers, proclaim curses against wrongdoers, make animal sacrifices, and discuss and vote on various civic and political issues.[7]

We can see this political aspect of *ekklēsia* at play in the book of Acts. When Paul and his companions were in Ephesus, their preaching nearly started a riot. The leading citizens of the city rushed into the theater and held an "assembly" (*ekklēsia*) to determine what to do with these Christian rabble-rousers (19:32, 39–41). In other words, the pagan leaders called an *ekklēsia* to figure out what to do with Jesus' *ekklēsia*.

It is noteworthy, therefore, that Paul and other New Testament writers referred to the gathered body of believers as an *ekklēsia*. There were other terms they could have used, like *synagōgē* ("place of assembly") or *koinōnia* ("fellowship"). Instead, they deliberately chose *ekklēsia*—a word packed with political meaning.[8]

This is where our watered-down, de-politicized understanding of *church* can mislead us. It fogs up our interpretive lenses and prevents us from appreciating the true scandal of Paul's message. Paul didn't throw Ephesus into an uproar by doing "churchy" things, like preaching sermons about a private savior who touched hearts without touching politics. Rather, Paul proclaimed that Jesus is Lord, and this was a politically disruptive thing to say.

Paul's gospel, in fact, destabilized the entire economy of the city of Ephesus. People were converting to Christ and therefore leaving behind their idols, which is bad for business if you're an idol maker. According to one silversmith, "There is danger not only that our trade will lose its good name, but also that the temple of the great goddess Artemis will be discredited; and the goddess herself, who is worshiped throughout the province of Asia and the world, will be robbed of her divine majesty" (Acts 19:27). Paul's proclamation that Jesus is King was an affront to Artemis, the patron goddess of the city, who was believed to be the source of the city's economic success. Wealth and idolatry, and the idolatry of wealth, walked hand in hand. And the gospel Paul preached disrupted both religion and politics.

In the ancient world, there was no separation between religion and politics; they went together like butter on bread.[9] Artemis wasn't just some goddess that people in Ephesus worshipped in the privacy of their individual lives. Rather, the Ephesians believed that their city's political success was intertwined with their devotion to Artemis.[10] If Artemis lost followers or didn't receive the homage she was due, she would remove her blessing from the city. This was what threw the city into a panic.

How should we, as exiles, interact with and respond to the politics of the empire?

Like the Hebrew exiles before them (Jer. 29:7), the Ephesian Christians were called to seek the good of their city. But they weren't called to prop Jesus up next to Artemis (or Caesar) to form a dual allegiance. *Shalom* would be manifest in Ephesus when colonies of heaven carried out the divine mission to be a light to the nations, to practice and promote the upside-down values of Christ and become a faithful presence in the city. Yes, this might have an effect on your job, your bank account, and your reputation. High-status people might look down on you for hanging out with immigrants and women and slaves and such. The gospel might interrupt your vision of making Ephesus great again. But "the political task of Christians is to be the church," to embody an alternative way of life under the lordship of King Jesus.[11]

Paul's preaching in Ephesus wasn't the first time the gospel threw a city into an uproar. Luke tells us about a similar political upheaval in Thessalonica, where Paul was accused of "turn[ing] the world upside down" and "acting contrary to Caesar's decrees, saying that there is another king—Jesus" (Acts 17:6–7 CSB). If *Jesus* is king, then Caesar must not be. The Thessalonians interpreted the gospel through a political lens. And I don't think they misunderstood Paul.

Preaching sermons about how to pray or read the Bible typically doesn't cause cities to riot. But preaching the good news that Rome had enthroned a new King by crucifying him threatened the legitimacy of the existing empire. Belonging to an *ekklēsia* that publicly announced this message was politically subversive.

The first-century church wasn't an apolitical spiritual gathering where individual Christians left their Roman politics at the door and picked them back up on their way out. It certainly wasn't a place where Christians mounted a Roman flag next to a Christian one. Rather, church was the foretaste of God's kingdom, a colony of heaven on earth. It was a place, a family, a gathering where God's plan for governing the world was being revealed and practiced, where participants submitted themselves to *God's* rule in realms like economics, immigration, bodily autonomy, war, violence, power, justice, and sexuality. Christians believed they were called to submit to governing authorities (Rom. 13:1–5). They also believed that governing authorities were empowered by Satan (Rev. 13:1–18) and would one day be destroyed by God (19:11–21).

But we're getting ahead of ourselves. I can already see some raised hands in the back. Even though we'll wrestle with some contemporary political questions in this book, my main goal is to lay a thick biblical foundation for constructing a Christian political identity. How should we, as exiles, interact with and respond to the politics of the empire? Before we address today's political environment, we need to understand why a peace-preaching Jew living on the fringes of the Roman Empire was crucified for treason and how a Jew from Tarsus could be accused of turning the world upside down by telling people about Jesus. Before looking at the crater

Jesus left in the political world, we'll venture back even further to the formation of the nation of Israel, followed by the moment when "exile" became a political identity for the people of God.

What This Book Is About

As we begin our historical investigation, let me offer four clarifications of what this book is all about.

First, my focus will be on what scholars call biblical theology or exegetical theology. This isn't primarily a work of political theology. Political theology is its own discipline, and while I've benefited much from political theology scholars, I don't claim to be one of them.[12] I'm first and foremost an exegete—an interpreter of Scripture—so this is the lane I want to stay in. I'll explore some implications of our exegesis for political theology in chapters 9 and 10, but I'll do so cautiously.

Second, with this exegetical focus in mind, one of my goals is to show that huge swaths of Scripture are political in nature. (I'll define *political* below.) Not only do nations and empires play a significant role in the storyline of Scripture, but the gospel itself is profoundly political—just not in the way many partisan-minded Christians think it is. There's a saying that goes, "The gospel is political but not partisan," and I agree. Scripture should, of course, determine how we view political questions today (immigration, warfare, racism, economics, sexuality, etc.). But Scripture also warns against letting our hearts become co-opted by the kingdoms of this earth. If I can be frank, I think a massive problem in the church today, especially in the United States, is that Christians hold the Bible in one hand

and secular politics in the other. We fail to let the former (the Bible) shape the latter (our politics). Or, even worse, we form opinions about secular politics and *then* go back to the Bible and use it to rubber-stamp our pre-formed political views. Just take how some Christians seem more passionate about the Second Amendment than the second commandment. (Knowing what the former is and not the latter might illustrate the point.) Or think about how some Christians might react to questions like "Is it wrong to pledge allegiance to the American flag?" or "Does welfare help the poor or hurt them?" or "Are Christian nationalists more of a threat to society than Marxists?" or "Should Christians support America's military?" Even asking these questions might start a fight, especially in church. But is our anger around these topics fueled by the narrative of Scripture? Or are we motivated by one of America's partisan political tribes? I suspect that some of the political values we passionately cling to weren't unearthed by a steady study of Scripture but largely shaped by our current political parties and news outlets.

Part of the reason for this book, then, is to soak ourselves in the narrative of Scripture, with all its politically relevant themes, and let Scripture become the primary lens through which we interact with the politics of earthly empires.

Third, I want us to take (more) seriously the political implications of our allegiance to King Jesus. To put it plainly, I think "God and country" ideology cuts against the grain of Scripture and, in its more extreme forms, is idolatry. By "God and country," I mean the view that Christians should give their allegiance *both* to God *and* to their country—whatever country that may be. I'm not talking about submitting to governing authorities or being good citizens. The Bible clearly teaches that. I'm talking about allegiance. I'm talking about being more passionate about American values than Christian ones, or not knowing the difference. I'm talking about losing your mind when your favorite political leader doesn't get elected. And while the slogan "God and country" might evoke images of right-wing Christianity, I think the problem of dual allegiance exists on both sides of the political aisle.

Now, some of you might say, "Of course we shouldn't give *equal* allegiance to God and country; it's God first, country second." (I think even this approach is wrongheaded, as we'll see later.) And yet, though many American Christians say this, our lives often prove otherwise. Partisan politics have divided churches and friends and families *who are Christians*. This division suggests to me that our allegiance to the state is sometimes, in practice, stronger than our allegiance to Christ.

A couple of years ago, a friend of mine told me she was thankful that her unsaved neighbor couldn't make it to church. I thought it was strange for a Christian to be thankful that a non-Christian didn't come to church, but it made sense when my friend explained why. She had been building a relationship with her neighbor—who happened to be a Democrat—and finally asked if she'd be interested in visiting church with her. The neighbor said yes and was really excited to see what church was all about. But when Sunday rolled around, the neighbor told my friend that she was sick and couldn't make it. "I was disappointed at first," my friend told me. "But then, after hearing my pastor's sermon, I was actually thankful my neighbor couldn't be there." She went on to explain why: "My pastor happened to preach a sermon that was more about right-wing politics than about Jesus. Had my neighbor heard the sermon, she would have been shamed for being a Democrat. She would have believed that being a Christian meant voting Republican."

Instead of hearing that she was a sinner in need of grace, this woman would have heard that she was a Democrat in need of becoming a Republican. Which, of course, is heresy.

One of the goals of this book is to show that the dual-allegiance "God and country" view runs counter to how God's people viewed themselves throughout Scripture. The Jews living under Babylonian or Persian rule, or Christians living under Roman rule, would find our undiluted patriotism quite odd. Instead of a "God and country" lens, I want us to cultivate an exilic lens—one where we see ourselves as exiles taking up temporary residence in a modern-day Babylon.

Instead of hearing that she was a sinner in need of grace, this woman would have heard that she was a Democrat in need of becoming a Republican.

Fourth, this book isn't partisan. It's probably more anti-partisan than anything, though what I mean by that phrase will take the rest of this book to unpack. I may say things that challenge one side of the partisan aisle, but I'll also do the same with the other side. I do believe that numerically, the church (in the United States, at least) has a far greater problem with right-wing idolatry than left-wing. While the numbers are heavier on one side, however, I see political idolatry to be equally problematic on both sides. So please don't misunderstand any critique of the political right as support for the political left or vice versa.

Also, since I'm writing from the context of the United States, I'll frequently have this country in mind as I reflect on politics. I do hope that my reading of Scripture will be transferable to Christians living out their exile in other countries, especially other powerful countries like Russia, China, India, and the United Kingdom. Either way, for good or for ill, many people in the world are affected by the global influence of the United States, making my admittedly US context somewhat relevant for all Christians across the globe.

My Political Journey

Like most books, this one has a story behind it, which I suspect might be similar to some of yours. I was raised in a staunchly right-wing, conservative Christian environment. I believed that Christians voted Republican while non-Christians voted Democrat. Ronald Reagan possessed near-messianic status, and right-wing values were all equated with being a faithful Christian: opposing abortion; supporting the death penalty; being pro-military, anti-Communist, pro-guns, anti-homosexuality, anti-environmental-concerns, anti-anything-Democrats-say-and-believe. Put simply, left-wingers were our enemy.

Throughout my twenties and thirties, I slowly drifted away from this mindset. To be clear, I didn't conclude that all right-wing values are bad. I think some of these values resonate with Christianity, while others seem more American than biblical. But I began to see the danger of a partisan tribalism where everyone on the left is viewed as the enemy and right-wing political positions are equated with Christianity.

So I left Republican right-wing Christianity and peeked into the door of left-wing Christianity. Honestly, it looked eerily the same. I saw another set of values that resonated with the way of Jesus at times, but I also saw the same kind of tribalistic, anti-all-things-the-other-side-believes attitude that had driven me out of right-wing Christianity. In my experience, fundamentalism is an attitude that can exist equally on both the left and the right. The further you go on either side of the left/right spectrum, the stronger the fundamentalist tendencies: partisan groupthink governs your values, and members of the other party are no longer neighbors but enemies.

I've come to believe that, for Christians in America, allegiance to either the Republican right or the Democrat left is toxic. It divides the church, destroys our witness, and brings profound joy to the Devil, who's always looking for creative ways to derail the kingdom of God. Over the last ten years or so, I've been using the phrase "exile in Babylon" to describe a different kind of Christian political identity, a theological alternative to the toxic left/right options so many Christians have accepted.

It's important to note that my use of *exile* is very different from how some (usually right-wing) Christians might use the term to lament the fact that they no longer have power and influence in what used to be a "Christian nation." They see culture as having departed from its once-Christian roots, and the way to get back on track—to return from exile—is to vote Christians or conservatives into political office and take back the culture for God. I think this perspective is theologically anemic; it uses the language of exile but severs it from its biblical roots. And, to be honest, it feels a bit whiny to me. Like some rich teenager who just had his Tesla taken away. Anyway, it should be clear rather quickly that this brand of exile thinking is *not* what I'll be arguing for.

That brings us to this book. *Exiles* is an attempt to put biblical flesh on the idea that Christians should view ourselves as exiles living in the shadow of a foreign empire. This kind of perspective should cultivate a robust political identity *from which* we think through various political questions today. One of my ultimate goals—one that's pretty vanilla, if you think about it—is to shift our political conversations as Christians toward what the Bible actually says rather than what our favorite political pundits say. When faced with a question like "What's your view of immigration?" I want to see Christians intuitively *start* that conversation by considering what the Bible says about immigrants. Or the question, "Are you a capitalist or democratic socialist?" Rather than parroting what your favorite political party tells you to say, I want your knee-jerk reaction to be to look to the Bible. And the confidence of your response should match the depth of your study of Scripture on economics. It actually has much to say.

Viewing ourselves as exiles living under a foreign empire should strengthen the church's unity and group identity. Imagine a world where our common baptism into the death and resurrection of Jesus bonds us together much more than our political views. Imagine a world where you feel closer to a fellow believer who voted differently than you do to someone who shares your political leanings. Imagine a world where being left wing or right wing aren't the only options, where Christ's kingdom creates a whole different way of viewing politics. I fear that we've so absorbed the narratives of our political surroundings that they've stunted our political and theological imagination. Secular politics has created a playing field with only the Left and the Right, liberals and conservatives. "Which one are you?" people ask. "Are you left or right?" I long for the day when Christians confidently smile at this question and answer, "I'm diagonal."

To be clear, by renouncing the left/right political options and saying, "I'm diagonal," I am not at all arguing for a centrist or moderate position that exists somewhere between the left/right options. Centrists are defined by the same political grid, whereas I'm arguing for a different grid altogether—a political identity that doesn't derive from the secular left/center/right options. Exiles don't have to let Babylon (or any empire where they live) determine what their moral grid looks like or what categories are available.

Defining Our Terms

Before we jump in, a few quick definitions.

Political is a tricky word with many definitions. One of the most helpful and concise definitions I've found comes from theologians

William Cavanaugh and Peter Scott, who define *political* as "the use of structural power to organize a society or community of people."[13] I also like the way Timothy Gombis relates politics to the *polis*:

> Politics involves the proper ordering of social practices and relationships, and patterns of economic exchange within a social group.… Politics has to do with all sorts of behaviors in the *polis*. That term—*polis*—is the Greek term that denoted ancient cities and all that held them together as cohesive social and cultural units. The *polis* is the body politic, a gathered people regarded as a political body under an organized government. Politics, then, has to do with ruling and socially ordering a *polis*.[14]

An organized society, or *polis*, will develop certain approaches to resources (economics), leadership, who's allowed in and on what terms (citizenship, immigration, etc.), sexuality and marriage, how to defend the community against possible attacks (military and policing), legitimate uses of power, how we care for those who lack resources, and so on.[15] All this applies to how nations are organized—which is what most people think of when they hear the word *political*—but it also applies to any kind of society or community, including the church. This is what I mean when I say the church is political. More accurately, the church is theopolitical: its politics should be based on what God (*theos*) thinks about these matters.

I've also already used the term *Babylon*, which is the name of an ancient city and nation. But in Judeo-Christian tradition, the term *Babylon* came to apply not just to the ancient city and the whole Babylonian Empire but to all nations and empires on earth that are Babylon-like, especially ones that are very wealthy, powerful, militaristic, and oppressive.[16] I'll spend a good deal of time unpacking this metaphorical (or, more precisely, metonymic) use of *Babylon* in chapters 3 and 8.

Empire is another term that's defined in rather extreme ways. Some people use the term so narrowly that you practically need to build a Death Star to count as an empire. Others use the term so broadly that nearly everything can be an empire. Indeed, whole books have been written to define and explain the notion of empire. I like Peter Leithart's description of *empire* as "a particular distribution of international political power." He goes on to explain that the terms *empire* and *imperial*

> refer loosely to certain formal political structures in which one people, kingdom, or nation *exercises dominance over or otherwise leads and guides and shapes another nation or people.* Sometimes, the "imperial" nation forces another nation or nations to do its bidding by violence, threats of violence, economic manipulations, or other tools of domination [but in other situations] one nation voluntarily submits itself to the leadership and protection of another nation and ... the imperial nation does not "dominate" the subordinate nation.[17]

By this definition, God's people found themselves living in several empires throughout Scripture: Babylon, Persia, Greece, and Rome.[18] I'm no political scientist, but according to Leithart's definition, the United States of America would also qualify as an empire, or at least as empire-like. It's hard to disagree with political theorist Samir Puri on this point:

> While the USA does not self-identify as an empire, it has become the embodiment of an informal empire. Its global reach includes: military bases dotted around the world; fleets of globally deployable aircraft carriers; strategic alliances on every continent; orbital satellites that guide missiles; technology innovations with global consumer appeal; and economic power underpinned by the USA dollar as the world's reserve currency. The USA can dominate many parts of the world, or at least it can make its influence telling. For now it remains *the* country that can intervene militarily virtually anywhere to defend its vision of world order, and its notions of right and wrong.[19]

This point isn't really debated among people who live outside the US. I recently asked my British friend Peter Williams if he thought the US was an empire. (As a Brit, Peter knows a thing or two about empire.) He looked at me like I'd asked him if 2 + 2 = 4.

As for the meaning of *exile*, it has too many layers and shades to cram into a single definition. It's a place, but not a place. It's a human state of being, but not a human state. It doesn't lament but *celebrates* its lack of worldly power. It's church, but more than church, and it certainly serves good coffee. It's an attitude, a theology, a posture, a political identity. Exile is bread and wine, resistance and submission, sacrifice and subversion. It seeks the good of the city, which sometimes throws the city into an uproar. Exile is enemy love, cultural weakness, and divine power that is shaped by the sacrificial self-giving of King Jesus.

I mean, it really is hard to define. It takes a whole book to unpack and a lifetime to embrace, which is what I hope to help us do in the pages that follow, beginning with Israel's upside-down kingdom and how this relates to living as exiles in the shadow of empire.

Chapter 2

ISRAEL'S UPSIDE-DOWN KINGDOM

From Israel's inception, God designed his people to be set apart, to be not like the other nations. Israel's most unique feature was its belief in one God named Yahweh who ruled the world. But Israel's monotheism wasn't the only thing that set it apart. Israel was also called to be politically different from other nations. In terms of its design, though not always its actual practice, the nation of Israel was set up to be a countercultural, upside-down, hardly recognizable kingdom.[1]

This doesn't mean Israel was completely otherworldly. It was an ancient Near Eastern nation that held many cultural, social, and even ethical beliefs in common with other nations. But the fundamental political values embedded in various laws and institutions made Israel stand out as different, perhaps even backward or peculiar, as the wayward prophet Balaam once said, "I see a people

who live apart and do not consider themselves one of the nations"
(Num. 23:9).[2]

In this chapter, we'll refract Israel's distinct political identity
through four lenses: (1) kingship, (2) militarism, (3) economics, and
(4) social class and power. This list isn't comprehensive; there are
many other sociopolitical values that set Israel apart.[3] But compre-
hensiveness isn't my goal here. Rather, I want to survey examples
of Israel's countercultural politics to illustrate the point that God's
people have always been called to embody an upside-down kingdom—even when they *were* an actual earthly kingdom.

The Upside-Down Kingdom

If Israel had followed God's political design, it would have looked
very different from the surrounding nations. Nowhere is this more
apparent than in its approach to kingship.

KINGSHIP

Kingship was vital for the success of any nation in the ancient world.
Maybe this is why the kind of king God planned for Israel was virtually unrecognizable by any ancient Near Eastern standard.

Archaeological and literary evidence from Mesopotamia, Egypt,
and Canaan shows that the nations surrounding ancient Israel
invested a lot of trust in the power of their kings.[4] They were viewed
as divine (or semi-divine) representatives of gods and were expected
to possess loads of power, which was displayed through large harems
and excessive wealth and by gobbling up huge tracks of land.

To protect and extend their power, ancient kings were expected to build and sustain a strong military. A highly trained standing army was a must: the bigger, the better. Powerful militaries were a source of much boasting in the ancient world. A strong military could ward off external threats and expand their empire (which led to more wealth). Particularly violent militaries, like Assyria's, sent waves of fear across the lands they sought to conquer. You might think twice about opposing an army if you'd heard they would skin you alive and prop your severed head on a pole.

In striking contrast, God's blueprint for kingship in Israel reads like a mirror-opposite script from what we see among other nations. According to Deuteronomy 17,

> The king ... must not acquire great numbers of horses for himself or make the people return to Egypt to get more of them, for the LORD has told you, "You are not to go back that way again." He must not take many wives, or his heart will be led astray. He must not accumulate large amounts of silver and gold. (vv. 16–17)

You can almost hear other nations laughing at this point. It's as if God was taking another nation's blueprint for kingship and turning it inside out. As Joshua Berman writes, "The limitations of the Israelite king ... are without parallel in the ancient Near East. Nowhere else do we find legal curbs on the size of the military, the treasury, and the harem."[5]

The command that the king "must not take many wives, or his heart will be led astray" (v. 17) is primarily aimed against making political alliances with other nations through marriage. This practice was common in the ancient world, but it almost always led to the introduction of foreign deities (Deut. 7:3–5), which is exactly what happened when Israel's kings violated this command (1 Kings 11:1–13).

Israel's king also "must not accumulate large amounts of silver and gold" (Deut. 17:17), which is precisely what kings of other nations *would* do. Wealth was a sign of status and power; the more wealth, the more power. Limiting the king's wealth put a "limit on the king's accumulation of power and status above other Israelites."[6] This is why God said that the king must be "from among your fellow Israelites" and must "not consider himself better than his fellow Israelites" (Deut. 17:15, 20). Telling a king to think no more highly of himself than of anyone else was like telling him he wasn't really a king—which might be precisely God's point in Deuteronomy 17. *God* was the king over Israel, the nations, and all creation.[7] The human king was to lead in humble obedience to his Creator, modeling how every Israelite was to live.[8] He was commanded to follow the law just like everyone else. Unlike other kings—who were either above the law or, in the case of Babylon's Hammurabi, the creator of the law—Israel's king was to submit to God's law and "to read it all the days of his life so that he may learn to revere the LORD his God and follow carefully all the words of this law and these decrees" (v. 19).[9] Leaders in God's upside-down kingdom—even kings—are no better than anyone else.

God also took away the king's military by saying he "must not acquire great numbers of horses for himself or make the people return to Egypt to get more of them" (v. 16). God didn't have anything against horses per se; he wasn't equinophobic. In ancient warfare, the number of horses determined the strength of an army. In fact, "warhorses" might be the best translation here. Unlike the kings of Egypt and Mesopotamia, Israel's king was commanded *not* to build a strong military and not to make military alliances with other nations.

Deuteronomy 17 seeks to create an anti-kingly king stripped of all sources of pomp and pride. True power would come with living a humble life in submission to the real King of Israel.

God's upside-down vision for kingship in Israel was reemphasized when Israel deliberately went against it. In 1 Samuel 8, the Israelites went to Samuel the prophet and told him to "appoint a king to lead us, *such as all the other nations have*" (v. 5). Samuel told them exactly what this king-like-the-nations would be like (vv. 10–18). He would draft Israel's sons into a standing army to drive his chariots and warhorses. He'd take their women to serve in his fields and in his kitchen. He'd take their land and their wealth, and "you yourselves will become his slaves" (v. 17). Israel responded, "We want a king over us. Then we will be *like all the other nations*, with a king to lead us and to go out before us and fight our battles" (vv. 19–20).

Instead of choosing a humble, nonmilitaristic, Deuteronomy 17 king, Israel wanted a power-mongering king who looked just like the kings of the nations. But God designed Israel's monarchy to be *upside down.*

MILITARISM

In the ancient world, kingship and military might went together like hot dogs and baseball. Highly successful kings didn't simply defend their borders; they expanded them. They didn't just ward off their enemies; they built empires. Israel, in contrast, was designed to be a demilitarized nation, and empire building was considered a moral evil.

The Old Testament's demilitarization of kingship, which we've just explored, was part of a larger worldview regarding military strength. Some people assume that the Old Testament was highly militaristic, since Israel seems to wage war all over the place. After all, didn't God himself tell Israel to go to war—even to annihilate whole populations (e.g., Deut. 20:16–17)?

The nature of God's involvement with Israel's wars is debated. But even if we assume that God did command Israel to engage in at least some wars, one thing is clear: God was always against *militarism*.

Militarism is defined as "the belief or policy that a country should maintain a strong military capability and be prepared to use it aggressively to defend or promote national interests."[10] In other words, a nation that is militaristic must have a standing army—the bigger, the better—and be ready to wield it in self-defense or to extend the empire. *Militarism* is a perfect description of many nations in Israel's day. The Egyptians, the Babylonians, the Hittites, and especially the Assyrians celebrated—one might say idolized—the military strength wielded by their kings. But Israel? Israel was prohibited from even having a standing army. Deuteronomy's description of Israel's military policy is almost comical. "When you are about to go into battle," God said, "the priest shall come forward and address the army" (20:2). After the priests were done, the officers were to whittle down the size of the military by giving this speech:

> "Has anyone built a new house and not yet begun to live in it? Let him go home, or he may die in battle and someone else may begin to live in it. Has anyone planted a vineyard and not begun to enjoy it? Let him go home, or he may die in battle and someone else enjoy it. Has anyone become pledged to a woman and not married her? Let him go home, or he may die in battle and someone else marry her." Then the officers shall add, "Is anyone afraid or fainthearted? Let him go home so that his fellow soldiers will not become disheartened too."
> (vv. 5–8)

New homeowners, newly betrothed, anyone who had planted a vineyard and not yet enjoyed its wine (which takes about five to seven years from seed to glass), or anyone who was simply "afraid or fainthearted" could stay home and sit this one out. (I'd love to be a fly on the wall of a general's office today if a private tried to use one of these excuses.) Along with these exemptions from military service, the final order is to "appoint commanders over" the army on the spot (v. 9). "It is apparent from this verse," writes Old Testament scholar Peter Craigie, "that there is no conception of a permanent standing army, with regular officers and soldiers."[11] Israel's military was essentially a group of volunteers who were invited "to give virtually any excuse for not serving in a battle."[12] Why? Because "the LORD your God is the one who goes with you to fight for you against your enemies to give you victory" (v. 4).

Far from an all-hands-on-deck approach where strength is in numbers, Israel's success in war rested not on their army's size, skill, or superior weapons but on Yahweh, who fought for them (v. 1). Deep in the Old Testament, we already see shadows of a cross forming as worldly power is turned on its head.

In God's upside-down kingdom, things aren't always the way they seem. Lions rule the land. But sometimes lambs are more powerful than lions.

The Old Testament often highlights Israel's military weakness, most memorably in the story of Gideon, whose army was trimmed down from thirty-two thousand to three hundred. When they went into battle, they defeated the Midianites by blowing trumpets and smashing pots, causing their enemies to kill themselves (Judg. 7). Likewise, the Israelites stood by and watched God defeat Pharaoh's mighty army by drowning them in the Red Sea (Ex. 14). Hezekiah discovered, when the ruthless Assyrians were pounding at the gates, that prayer was more effective than making political alliances with other nations (2 Kings 18–19). Jehoshaphat prepped for battle by praying and singing worship songs, only to find the enemy dead when his army reached the battlefield (2 Chron. 20). Barak watched a Canaanite army stocked with nine hundred iron chariots fall to the power of Yahweh through the leadership of Deborah and a tent-peg-wielding woman named Jael (Judg. 4–5).

The Old Testament's project of demilitarization is seen clearly in its aversion to using chariots and warhorses, which were advanced weaponry in the ancient world. "A warrior is not delivered by his great strength," sang the psalmist. "The war horse is a false hope for salvation, and by its great might it cannot rescue" (33:16–17 ESV). God told the Israelites not to be afraid when they "see horses and chariots and an army greater than yours" (Deut. 20:1). Throughout the Old Testament, chariots and warhorses were either banned or simply mocked as false hope for victory. Israel was commanded to burn their enemies' chariots and hamstring their horses after a victory.[13] This made it impossible for them to add the enemies' superior weapons to the Israelite "military."

A lot of violence occurred in the Old Testament; some of it was even commanded by God (e.g., Deut. 20:16–17). But through it all, God constantly ordered his people to repudiate militarism.

What a contrast with the surrounding nations, which put great faith in (and money into) building standing armies and supplying them with superior weaponry. One Assyrian king boasted of terrifying his enemies, who were "afraid in the face of my terrible weapons."

Assyrians were widely known for their ruthless military tactics: skinning people alive, building piles of human skulls outside city gates, and ripping off the testicles of opposing soldiers "like seeds of a cucumber in June."[14] In terms of advanced military machinery, it was the Egyptians and Hittites who were known for stockpiling as many chariots as they could. Their battle against each other at Kadesh in 1274 BC went down as the largest chariot battle in ancient history. Interestingly, as in some recent American elections, both sides claimed victory.

Militarism also had a tremendous impact on a nation's economy and class distinctions. "To wage war required the necessary wealth, technology, and operating skill to create and sustain an effective chariot force," writes Old Testament scholar Norman Gottwald. "It elevated a class of military warriors and bureaucrats and depressed the larger population in subservience to them. To build and support the enlarged military establishment, heavier taxation in kind became necessary and larger public building projects had to be undertaken with forced labor."[15] Militarism feeds off economic exploitation, and it's always the poor who feel it the most. Some things, of course, never change.

Militarism makes sense from a right-side-up kingdom perspective. "Speak softly and carry a big stick," Teddy Roosevelt used to say. Assyria's slogan was something like "Speak loudly, say arrogant and dehumanizing things, and also carry a big stick, a massive sword, and a sharp knife for skinning your opponents." Either way, the big stick is important. It's logical to fight power with more of the same power. But in God's upside-down kingdom, things aren't always the way they seem. Lions rule the land. But sometimes lambs are more powerful than lions.

ECONOMICS

Ancient Near Eastern societies were built on a hierarchy of wealth. A few elites at the top held nearly all the wealth, while the masses below languished in poverty. Israel, however, was intended to be much more equal, a place where hierarchies based on social class were nearly abolished and common people had access to wealth. This intentional attempt to level the playing field came through Israel's economic system, which directly contrasted with that of other ancient Near Eastern nations.

In agrarian cultures, land was capital, and access to land was the way people gained wealth. No land, no money. Landless people lived in servitude, working on someone else's land.[16] Throughout the ancient world, kings and elites owned all the land, which became the bricks that formed economic pyramids of social hierarchies, where a few people at the top held power over the masses down below.

For instance, in Egypt, kings and priests owned almost all the land.[17] In Canaan, local kings owned the land, while "the rest of the population lived as peasant-tenants on land not their own, paying taxes and serving in the king's army."[18] Similarly, in Ugarit (north of Canaan), the royal court owned the land and paid peasants to work it.[19]

In Israel, however, the land was evenly distributed among the people "according to their families" (Josh. 13–19 NASB). The larger the tribe, the more land it received. In contrast to the hierarchical systems of other nations, Israel's kings and priests had no power over the land. They couldn't hold agricultural land, which is why they depended on the tithes and offerings of the people.[20] Instead of holding power *over* the people, Israelite priests depended on the power *of* the people. "Such decentralized power stands in marked contrast to contemporary ancient Near Eastern states which had highly stratified and pyramidical political and economic structures."[21]

Old Testament law also guaranteed that the land would stay in the hands of the people. Sometimes land was unable to yield produce because of drought or other natural disasters, forcing owners to sell it in order to survive. Old Testament law ensured that the owners would be able to buy it back when they were able (Lev. 25:25–28). Even if they were never able, the land would be returned to its original family owners in the Year of Jubilee (every fifty years).

In other cases, people who fell on hard times resorted to hiring themselves out as servant workers on someone else's land. The law demanded that these servants be released from their service after six years (Ex. 21:2). In the Year of Jubilee, all servants were released (Lev. 25:39–40). Like the land ownership laws, the purpose of these laws was to prevent powerful people from taking advantage of those in economic hardship.

Israel's economic system had many other countercultural features as well. In other nations, tithes and taxation went straight to the king, his military, the temple, and the state. In Israel, tithes supported the work of the temple and funded the priests and Levites, but they were also enjoyed by the people themselves (Deut. 14:22–26). Every third year, tithes went straight to the poor and disenfranchised (Deut. 14:27–29; 26:12–15).[22]

Interest rates on loans were another point of contrast between Israel and other nations. Rates typically ranged from 20 to 33 percent in other nations—sometimes as high as 80 percent—which allowed the wealthy to take advantage of those who fell on hard times.[23] The Old Testament, however, prohibits charging interest out of concern for the poor.[24] Israel's law contained several other pieces of legislation aimed at preventing the disenfranchised from falling into endless cycles of poverty: the release of debt (Deut. 15:1–7), the redemption of land previously sold (Lev. 25:8–28), and the mandatory release of slaves even if they hadn't fully paid off their debt.[25]

This upside-down economic system was rooted in the fundamental theological truth that God owned the land and the Israelites were simply guests in God's land: "The land ... is *mine*," said the Lord, "and you are only aliens and temporary residents on my land" (Lev. 25:23 CSB). God's people, in other words, were to live almost as if they were already exiles—living in a land that wasn't actually theirs—even when they were a nation-state with a geopolitical claim on the land. King Yahweh also reminded Israel over and over that they had all been impoverished slaves when he redeemed them and gave them the land. He reminded them not to think too highly of themselves and to care for those in need.

Israel didn't always live out God's economic design, however. Not long after the monarchy was established, the rich and powerful took advantage of the poor. King Ahab tried to take Naboth's vineyard and was severely rebuked by the prophet Elijah (1 Kings 21). Isaiah too condemned rich landowners who endlessly gobbled up surrounding land, sending other families into cycles of poverty (Isa. 5:8). Israel's prophets launched frequent attacks on the rich and powerful for taking advantage of the poor.[26] These prophets spoke not from high positions of social power but simply because they had been called by God—a dynamic unheard of in other nations, which listened only to prophets with power.

> When Christians think about money and economics, we need to stop letting the rhetoric and categories of Babylon's culture wars shape our values.

Social justice. Concern for the poor. Economic checks on the rich. Redistribution of wealth. Forgiveness of debt. These aren't liberal or Marxist or "woke" ideals. They're straight out of the Bible. So are other values like small governments, limits on centralized power, and able-bodied people working hard and saving for the future. When Christians think about money and economics, we need to stop letting the rhetoric and categories of Babylon's culture wars shape our values. The Bible provides us with some rich categories for thinking about these things.

Israel's economic system was designed to be different from that of the nations, since Israel's kingdom was an upside-down one.

Social Class and Power

The final lens we'll look at flows from the first three. Israel rejected the hierarchical pyramid of power divided among social classes that was pervasive in other Near Eastern societies. By "power," I mean "the ability to influence or coerce the behavior of others," which is "usually backed by the threat of force."[27] Like most societies today, ancient Near Eastern societies typically operated along the lines of social hierarchy, with higher social classes holding power over lower classes. But God had a different plan for his people.

We see this rejection of hierarchy most clearly in the case of Israel's priests, who were stripped of their power. As we noted earlier in this chapter, every tribe in Israel was allotted land in proportion to its needs, but priests (from the tribe of Levi) were excluded from the land allocation. Instead, they were dependent on the tithes and offerings of the people. In an agrarian society, not having land rights was a huge obstacle to amassing wealth and wielding power. Spiritual leaders like priests, both in the ancient world and in the present day, battle a unique temptation to use their spiritual authority to gain power over the people they're called to serve. Making priests *dependent* on the people they minister to reinforces their call to serve people rather than exploit them. Scripture goes so far as to include priests among the underprivileged—along with foreigners, orphans, and widows—highlighting their humble position as servants of the Lord (Deut. 14:29).

The Israelite priesthood looked quite different from that of other nations. In Egypt, for instance, priests not only owned land but also could amass great wealth and power—sometimes as much as the king, who himself accumulated massive fortunes.[28] The king appointed the high priest, creating a kind of ancient "good ol' boys club" at the top of the social pyramid.[29] In Israel, however, the high priest belonged to a tribe stripped of land rights and privilege. It's almost as if God knew from the beginning that humans are prone to abuse their spiritual authority and take advantage of the people they serve.

Ancient Israel also guarded against abuses of power in the judicial sphere. Instead of judges coming from an elite class or from among the king's cronies, as they did in the nations neighboring Israel, Deuteronomy says *the people* had the power to appoint judges. Since the people appointed judges, the community as a whole was held responsible to pursue justice in the courts, since the judges were representative of the people:

> *You* shall appoint for yourself judges and officers in all your towns. … *You* shall not distort justice, *you* shall not show partiality; and *you* shall not accept a bribe, because a bribe blinds the eyes of the wise and distorts the words of the righteous. Justice, and only justice, *you* shall pursue. (Deut. 16:18–20 NASB)

Like priests' and judges' power, prophets' power was also curbed in Israel's upside-down kingdom. On the one hand, Israelite prophets had a kind of spiritual power over the priests and even the king, which itself was countercultural. But on the other hand, the prophets were selected from among the common people: "The LORD your God will raise up for you a prophet like me from *among you*, from *your fellow Israelites*" (Deut. 18:15). This implies that "he is not the member of any elite lineage, does not possess inherent powers, but rather, an ordinary citizen."[30]

When it came to social class and power, Israel stood out as unique among its contemporaries. Skepticism about economically gargantuan governmental power didn't originate with modern conservatives, and rejection of wealth gaps and unequal hierarchies didn't originate with modern liberals. These concerns were written into God's vision for Israel.[31]

Kingdom of Priests

Even when God's people were a nation, they were a rather strange one. This wasn't a punk rock attempt to be different for the sake of difference. Israel's upside-down values had a missional purpose of reaching the nations.

This nation with an anti-kingly king, a demilitarized military, an egalitarian socioeconomic structure, and social systems that stripped power from the powerful was intended to show other nations a better way to live. Its logic was rooted in Genesis 1:27, where *everyone* is created in God's image. From welcoming a Canaanite harlot into their community, to caring for a Moabite widow on the edge of poverty, to praising humble leaders who submitted to God while lambasting kings who expanded the empire—Israel was stamped with a unique way of being human, showing the world what life was like in Eden.

This is why the entire countercultural law code of the Old Testament is prefaced with a mission statement. God created Israel to be "a kingdom of priests and a holy nation" (Ex. 19:6), what Isaiah called "a light to the nations" (49:6 NRSVUE). Israel's holiness, which included their distinctive socioeconomics and politics, had a priestly function. It was intended to show the world a better way to flourish in God's creation.

New Testament writers seamlessly wove Israel's vocation into the mission of the church. Stripped of land and earthly power, the global church finds itself living among the nations, still bearing God's mission to be "a kingdom of priests" and "a light to the nations."[32] The church too has a vocation of holiness. Its distinct, set-apart way of living in the world isn't inwardly focused or an end in itself. "The purpose is not to separate the 'pure' people from the 'impure' people, but rather to maintain a nonconformity to the world *as the basis from which to work for change*."[33] Holiness is always missional. To be a light to the nations, the church will need to live differently from the nations, not just in personal holiness but in sociopolitical holiness.

The New Testament church didn't ditch Israel's upside-down political paradigm. It refracted this paradigm through another lens—the lens of exile.

Chapter 3

EXILED TO BABYLON

Babylon. It's a city, a nation, and a concept. The ancient city lies in ruins in modern-day Iraq, but the concept of Babylon lives on. Throughout the Bible, Babylon symbolizes arrogant attempts to rule the world without God through power and oppression.[1]

We first hear about Babylon in Genesis 10, when a powerful hunter named Nimrod established a "kingdom" in "Babylon … in the land of Shinar" (vv. 8–10 CSB). The text feels the need to use the word *powerful* three times to describe Nimrod, which, according to Peter Leithart, "tantalizingly suggests that imperial power—rule of a people or city by another—is inherent in political order."[2] Whatever is implied of Nimrod's Babylon, the Bible frames it in a negative light. Nimrod's power is a source of suspicion, not praise. When Babylon is revisited in the next chapter, it's clearly opposed to God's way of ruling the world.

The Tower of Babel episode in Genesis 11 is a stunning critique of imperial power and oppression. (While most English translations distinguish between "Babel" and "Babylon," Hebrew has one word for both: *babel*.) Theologically, the story targets the evils of an imperial Babylonian ideology in at least four ways.

First, the builders of the tower are described as being "one people all having the same language" (v. 6 CSB), which is juxtaposed with the diverse nations and many languages of Genesis 10 (vv. 5, 20, 31–32). Hunkering down as one people, one nation, one language, in one part of creation went against God's original plan for humanity to spread out and fill the earth (Gen. 1:28). The repeated use of the word "one," four times in 11:1 and 11:6, "emphasizes that [Babel's] aim was uniformity."[3] As John Howard Yoder points out,

> The intention of the people at Babel was to resist the diversification which God had long before ordained and initiated, and to maintain a common discourse by building their own unprecedentedly centralized city. They were the first foundationalists, seeking by purposive focusing of their own cultural power to overcome historically developing diversity.[4]

Second, Babel's emphasis on "one language" represents the ancient policy "of indoctrinating foreigners into their supposedly superior language and culture."[5] We see evidence of such imperial propaganda in ancient inscriptions from the same area, where various kings would impose a single language on the people they conquered.[6] Such an oppressive attempt at forming a monolithic culture went against God's creative design and celebration of diversity. God's confusion of languages, then, was both punitive and restorative—a restoration that climaxed at Pentecost, which reversed Babel by creating unity *through* celebrating many diverse tongues (Acts 2).

Third, the author of Genesis 11 could have taken issue with the religious idolatry that pervaded ancient Babylon, but such religious critique is surprisingly absent. "Just when we would expect a frontal attack on … Mesopotamian religion," writes J. Richard Middleton, "we find instead a very secular, even humanistic account of the origin of this imperial civilization." That is, Genesis 11 exposes "the underlying human impulse to exercise power over others."[7] As Middleton goes on to point out, when Old Testament prophets critiqued Babylon, they did not "single out cultic practices, but rather imperial hubris, military fortifications, and oppressive power."[8]

Fourth, the theme of oppression is teased out when we notice the subtle connections to a later story: Pharaoh's brutal treatment of the Israelite slaves (Ex. 1–5). Both stories talk of mud bricks used in self-aggrandizing building projects. Both contain a similar call from the builders: "Come, let us build … lest we be scattered" (Gen. 11:4 NKJV) and "Come, let us deal shrewdly with them, lest they multiply" (Ex. 1:10 NKJV). And both stories try to halt God's plan for people to "increase in number [and] fill the earth" (Gen. 1:28).

The Tower of Babel episode, then, shows that God isn't on the side of one kind of people—one nation, one empire, one ethnic group. He is for the nations. And he is particularly opposed to civilizations that glory in their efforts to make a name for themselves.

Celebrating the greatness of one nation is a dangerous business, especially if the greatness of that nation was built on the backs of an oppressed—indeed, enslaved—people.

Babylon would go on to become an epicenter of cultural progress throughout the third and second millennia BC. It was in southern Babylonia—Ur of the Chaldeans—that God called Abram to leave his homeland and become "a foreigner in the land of promise," a "temporary [resident] on the earth" (Heb. 11:9, 13 CSB).[9] Abram left flourishing Babylon and took on his new identity as an exile in Canaan.

Following Abram's departure, the Bible falls silent about Babylon for many years. More than a thousand years later, God accommodated the Israelites' request for a king like the kings of the nations by giving them Saul (1 Sam. 8–9). With their own land and a king to rule over it, Israel became a kingdom. Not long afterward, the kingdom was divided between north and south, a division that lasted for a couple of hundred years. Neither the south nor (especially) the north embodied God's call to be "a kingdom of priests and a holy nation" (Ex. 19:6). Instead, they became like the nations around them.

Many of Israel's kings became wealthy, power-mongering, militaristic leaders who failed to embody the countercultural Deuteronomy 17 vision. The rest of Israel followed suit. Priests became gorged with power.[10] Violations of land policies ran rampant. Judicial leaders played favorites. The rich amassed power, the poor were oppressed, and sexual practices looked no different from those of the nations around them. God finally made good on his promise to punish the Israelites by sending them into exile, and he chose Babylon to be his servant—to do his bidding as an agent of exile.

Fresh off a decisive victory over Assyria in the east, mighty Babylon headed west to subjugate the southern kingdom of Israel (known as Judah). From 605 to 586 BC, Babylon conquered Judah. People were raped, starved to death, and forced to eat their own children during the Babylonian siege.[11] The temple was razed to the ground, shattering the faith of many. Some survivors were left in the barely inhabitable land. The ones who weren't killed or left behind were exiled to Babylon.

The Exile

The exile was a catastrophic *historical* event. To watch family and friends be slaughtered before their eyes, to witness foreigners burn God's residence to the ground, to be stripped from the only land they'd known—a land supposedly promised to them by God—left an indelible mark on the people of Israel. Whatever national identity they had was radically reconfigured.

The biblical exile was also a profound *theological* event. Nearly a thousand years prior, God made a covenant with the nation, promising to bless them if they obeyed and curse them if they didn't (Deut. 27–28). Though some obeyed some of the time, most didn't most of the time. So God used Babylon, whom Jeremiah called God's "servant" (27:6), to carry out the ultimate curse of the covenant: the curse of exile. Exile was God's theological response to Israel's persistent disobedience—just as, back in Genesis, exile from the garden of Eden was God's response to the disobedience of Adam and Eve.

Finally, exile was a significant *political* event. The Jewish people would now live as strangers and aliens under foreign rule. Babylon's policies for exiles were aimed at breaking the bonds of national identity and cultivating submission (and allegiance) to the Babylonian Empire. They did this by ripping people out of their land and saturating them with a steady stream of propaganda.[12] Exiles added numbers to Babylon's military and strengthened Babylon's economy.

Still, exile could have been worse for the Jewish people. Some exiles didn't have it all that bad, especially those who assimilated to the Babylonian way of life.[13] In fact, archaeological evidence shows that some Jews became quite wealthy and lived comfortable lives in Babylon.[14] This is probably why, when Persia conquered Babylon and allowed the exiles to return home, many Jews chose to stay in Babylon. Perhaps they viewed themselves no longer as Jewish exiles in Babylon but simply as Jewish Babylonians. (Some Christian Americans might not appreciate the problem.)

In any case, living in exile cultivated a distinct political identity. Stripped of land, king, and autonomous rule, Jewish exiles learned how to be a faithful presence in an empire not their own. As such, they had to negotiate at least four challenges.

First, they had to navigate imperial ideology. As Jon Berquist writes, "Empires dominate not only by military and economic means, but also through ideology."[15] The power of Babylon was advertised everywhere. Through propaganda in temples and shrines, art and architecture, literature and stories, Babylon elicited allegiance—or at least compliance. It's debated whether Babylon forced their religion on the Jewish exiles. Certainly, there was social pressure to give homage to Babylon's deities; the book of Daniel records an instance where Jews were forced to bow the knee to Babylon (Dan. 3). Whether they responded with compromise or resistance, the Jewish exiles woke up every day immersed in the narrative of Babylon's dominance over the Jews.[16]

Second, the exiles struggled to maintain religious and political purity. Remember, there was no division between religion and politics in ancient cultures.[17] To be political was to be religious; to be religious was to be political. It was the favor of the gods that ensured the political success of the nation. No ancient person—certainly not the Hebrew exiles—would have had a category for the modern person holding politics in one hand and religion in the other. Today people tend to read the stories of the fiery furnace and the lions' den as calls to resist spiritual idolatry, but ancients understood a deeper truth: resisting national idols meant resisting national allegiance. Refusal to bow the knee to Bel wasn't merely a matter of personal worship. It was treason.

Third, the exiles were constantly reminded that they were foreign minorities in a dominant culture. "A significant dynamic of the experience of Israel in Exile," writes Daniel Smith-Christopher, "is their consciousness of being among 'foreigners,' *irrespective of the outward similarity*" between them and their Babylonian neighbors.[18] God had given the Jewish people a distinct political and social ethic. They ate different foods and believed different things about economics, immigration, kingship, and military power. This doesn't mean there wasn't any overlap in values; both cultures believed adultery was wrong, for instance. But the exiles were steeped in a countercultural sociopolitical ethic, where all people bear God's image and the king is no better than his neighbor. The exiles would now have to embody their distinct sociopolitical identity while living in the shadow of the empire.

Last, Israel awaited deliverance—a time when they could return home. Would the exiles take up arms to fight another holy war as in the days of Joshua? Or would God crush the empire and walk them through the sea like in the days of Moses? Or would there be another way? The hope of deliverance sparked a range of opinions among the exiles.

Seek the Peace of the City

The hope of deliverance lingers in the background of God's famous word to Jeremiah:

> Build houses and settle down; plant gardens and
> eat what they produce. Marry and have sons and
> daughters; find wives for your sons and give your
> daughters in marriage, so that they too may have
> sons and daughters. Increase in number there; do
> not decrease. Also, seek the peace and prosperity of
> the city to which I have carried you into exile. Pray
> to the LORD for it, because if it prospers, you too
> will prosper. (29:5–7)

Some people believe this passage supports a "God and country" theology, with exiles being commanded to worship Yahweh and also pledge allegiance to Babylon. But context shows that this passage isn't as pro-Babylon as it might seem.[19] The point of the passage is to tell God's people to prepare for a longer exile than they had hoped for. They were called to "seek the peace and prosperity of the city" because they were going to be there for a while.

The larger context of Jeremiah is important. Chapters 27–29 highlight the growing tension between two viewpoints. A prophet named Hananiah predicted a swift end to exile and impending return to the land of Israel. God "will break the yoke of Nebuchadnezzar king of Babylon off the neck of all the nations within two years," Hananiah prophesied (28:11; cf. vv. 2–3).[20] But Jeremiah knew exile would last much longer than expected—seventy years, to be exact (29:10; cf. 25:11). This is why he told the Israelites to "build houses and settle down."

Hananiah's "swift end to exile" perspective was likely fueled by visions of revolt. Daniel Smith-Christopher points out, "Most commentators assume that Hananiah was preaching some form of noncooperation and resistance to the Babylonian conquerors, perhaps with the assumed support of Egypt."[21] The Jews had solicited the help of Egypt to ward off the Babylonian army before; even though it hadn't worked, maybe this time would be different. Hananiah's call to the people is a call to be ready for war.

By telling people to "build houses and settle down," Jeremiah was doing just the opposite. You might recall that Deuteronomy 20 (Israel's anti-militaristic blueprint for warfare) allowed anyone who had *built* a house, *planted* a vineyard, or recently pledged to *marry* to be exempt from war. The Jews took this text quite seriously. Hundreds of years later, when Judas Maccabeus was about to go to war, he told "those who were *building houses* or were about to be *married* or were *planting* a vineyard ... to go home" (1 Maccabees

3:56 NRSVUE). As Smith-Christopher argues, "It is clear that Jeremiah is not simply advising a settled existence, but that he uses the Deuteronomic exemptions from warfare to declare an 'armistice' on the exile community."[22]

In short, Jeremiah was confronting a militaristic attitude brewing among the exiles. He was discouraging a violent revolt. Ironically, some modern interpreters use Jeremiah 29 as evidence that Christians should support a country's military—but Jeremiah's actual words are discouraging, not supporting, militaristic action.

Far from encouraging militarism, Jeremiah called the exiles to seek the peace (*shalom*) of the city and to "increase in number." *Shalom* in its most basic sense means "wholeness, completeness, cessation of war, and restoration of relationship." When combined with *prosperity* (v. 7), it often refers to material blessings alongside spiritual wholeness.[23] Economic justice, where the powerful don't oppress the poor, is a form of *shalom*. Throughout the Old Testament, *shalom* "is both a restoration of the divine plan of creation and the harbinger of the completion of life to come. And to the ears of a weary planet it brings the good news that strife shall cease and that the peoples of the earth 'shall beat their swords into plowshares and their spears into pruning hooks.'"[24]

The phrase "increase in number" recalls the many commands in Genesis to "be fruitful and *increase in number*" (1:28; cf. 1:22; 9:1, 7; 35:11). The Hebrew slaves in Egypt took this command seriously; they continued to be "exceedingly fruitful" and "increased in numbers" (Ex. 1:7; cf. 1:9, 20). Jeremiah's counsel to "increase in number" was a call to the Israelites not just to have sex and create babies but to keep their eyes fixed on the divine mission given to Adam, Eve, Noah, and Abraham—to extend God's rule to the ends of the earth. Being exiled doesn't stop us from carrying on God's mission.

There's nothing in the text suggesting that Jeremiah was advocating for patriotism toward Babylon here. He wasn't encouraging the exiles to place a Babylonian flag next to a star of David in their synagogues. He wasn't telling them to celebrate Babylon's powerful military, or to support a certain Babylonian leader who had a better economic policy, or to lose their minds over Babylonian leaders who wanted to see Babylon prosperous at all costs. The exiles were to seek the peace of Babylon *as exiles*, not as Babylonians. They were to maintain their distinct sociopolitical identity. Jeremiah wasn't commanding them to turn their upside-down values right side up. Rather, he was encouraging peaceful submission to an idolatrous nation *as* an expression of being an upside-down people. Don't revolt. Be patient. Trust God and wait. Cultivate a peaceful presence in the midst of a hostile nation. In due time, God is going to crush Babylon.

Empire in the Book of Daniel

In some ways, the book of Daniel reads like an extended commentary on Jeremiah's advice to "seek the peace and prosperity of the city." Here we have four Jewish boys living lives of obedience to God and submission to Babylon. But when submission competed with their allegiance to Yahweh, these radical exiles gladly chose death over compromise.

The book of Daniel is a treatise on both theological faithfulness *and* political subversion. Theology and politics are intertwined like threads in a rope. Babylon was described as a beast and its kingdom competed with Yahweh's rule over the earth, which is why faithfulness to Yahweh sometimes demanded disobedience to Babylon. The idea that believers could give their allegiance to both God and Babylon doesn't exist in the book of Daniel.

Central to the book of Daniel is the claim that God's messianic kingdom won't coexist alongside Babylon or any other kingdom in some kind of happy partnership.

If there is a single theme in Daniel, it has to do with the kingdom of God coming to earth. And *kingdom*, it's important to note, is a political term or, more precisely, a theopolitical term. The same term (*kingdom*) used to describe God's rule over the earth also describes earthly governments—specifically, Babylon, Persia, Greece, and Rome.[25]

Central to the book of Daniel is the claim that God's messianic kingdom won't coexist alongside Babylon or any other kingdom in some kind of happy partnership, nor will God's reign simply exist as some kind of invisible reality in the hearts and minds of God's people. Rather, God's kingdom "will *crush* all those kingdoms"— Babylon, Persia, Greece, and Rome—"and bring them to an end" (2:44). Earthly kingdoms aren't neutral entities. They are beasts who compete with God's rule over the earth. In his sovereignty, God allows them to stay in office for however long he wants them to be, and he even uses them to carry out his purpose on earth. But peel back the curtain and you will see that these beasts are demonically empowered (10:10–21). In due time, God will remove their authority, destroy them, and give their bodies over to burning fire as he sets up his multi-ethnic, upside-down kingdom ruled by the Son of Man. Daniel's terrifying vision says it all:

> I kept looking until the beast was slain and its body destroyed and thrown into the blazing fire. (The other beasts had been stripped of their authority, but were allowed to live for a period of time.)
>
> In my vision at night I looked, and there before me was one like a son of man, coming with the clouds of heaven. He approached the Ancient of Days and was led into his presence. He was given authority, glory and sovereign power; all nations and peoples of every language worshiped him. His dominion is an everlasting dominion that will not

pass away, and his kingdom is one that will never
be destroyed. (7:11–14)

One "like a son of man" receives a "kingdom" from "the
Ancient of Days"—a kingdom that consists of "peoples of every
language." This is a theme that will explode onto the scene in the
New Testament, where Jesus is the Son of Man who sets up a kingdom. Notice the political context of Jesus receiving his kingdom. It's
in response to God crushing earthly kingdoms. Kingdom replaces
kingdoms; God's empire takes over earthly empires. We'll see later
that this takeover isn't through violent revolt, taking back the culture for God, or any other power moves that imitate Babylon. The
Son of Man's kingdom is "not of this world," as Jesus made clear
(John 18:36).

But the concept of "kingdom" shouldn't be divorced from its
political connotations. There's one true way to rule the world, and
God will establish that rule through his messianic community. All
other attempts to rule God's world are blasphemy and destined to
destruction.

Daniel and his three friends were good citizens. They sought
the peace of the city and submitted to Babylon. Yet their exilic
identity forced them to peek behind the curtain and recognize
what Babylon really was. It wasn't a friend or an ally or a trust-
worthy partner in building God's kingdom. It was a demonically
empowered beast that would be destroyed. So were Persia, Greece,
Rome, and other empires to follow. The best way exiles can seek
the good of Babylon is by living lives of submissive subversion,

anticipating God's future triumph over the beastly empires competing with his reign.[26]

Excursus: The Synagogue as a Place of Submissive Protest

It was in exile that the Jews invented the synagogue, a place where faithful Jews could gather to worship, study, and cultivate the countercultural values of Israel. The synagogue "was the most fundamental sociological innovation in the history of religions."[27] There was no priest, no flash and flare, and no hierarchy. A trained rabbi might lead the community in the study of Scripture, but he didn't wield top-down authority. The synagogue was at the heart of the exiles' cultural and political identity. It was where exiles practiced Sabbath, ate meals according to their dietary laws, and practiced liturgies of study and worship that reinforced their countercultural uniqueness. The synagogue nurtured the group's identity of being strangers in a strange land.

Black churches in the United States have historically embodied a similar sociopolitical purpose, especially those formed while Jim Crow laws were still rigorously upheld. Centuries of slavery and ongoing racism create a kind of collective trauma, resulting in an ironclad resilience that comfortable people drunk on worldly power will never experience. Black churches weren't just houses of worship. They were also a space where marginalized people could celebrate their exilic identity, forged in the fires of oppression and exclusion.

Exilic gatherings were never designed to run on worldly systems of power. "The church in Babylon needs to organize itself according to its vision and not according to models of patriarchal, majority, powerful domination."[28] Churches that occupy positions of power (or wish they did) have a much harder time cultivating a theology of distinction and embodying an alternative way of living as a kingdom of priests to the nations. Powerful churches often share more in common with Babylon than they do with those who are exiled.

Still in Exile

Seventy years later, the Jewish exiles were allowed to return to their homeland. The Persian leader Cyrus the Great had conquered Babylon, and Persia had a more nuanced policy of rule than their predecessors. Scholars believe that the Persian Empire "allowed a considerable degree of social-cultural autonomy to subject peoples" and "never pressed a particularly Persian way of life onto subject peoples."[29] But this wasn't because they were altruistic. They were still an empire that dominated many people who stood in their way. Persia simply believed that ruling people with a heavy hand provoked unrest and revolt—and it didn't make people want to pay their taxes. Persia ruled the world through power and oppression; they were still a beast. But they found out that happy people pay their taxes on time.

Persia instituted a policy of return, allowing exiled peoples to go back to their homelands. They even funded the rebuilding of the Jewish temple in Jerusalem, completed a couple of decades after the exiles returned. Yet the Jews who returned to Israel quickly realized that though they had left Babylon, *they were still in exile.*

They weren't in physical exile—they weren't forcibly displaced. After all, they were back in the land. But it soon became clear that they were still in a sort of theopolitical exile.[30]

For one thing, the rebuilt temple didn't match the grandeur of Solomon's temple, which had been destroyed by Babylon. Worse still, the presence of God hadn't returned to the temple. While in exile, Ezekiel had seen the glory of God leave the temple just before it was destroyed (Ezek. 8–11) and envisioned that it would return when the temple was rebuilt (Ezek. 40–43). But that never happened. The glory didn't return. The lights were on in the new temple, but no one was home.

Plus, even though the exiles were back in their homeland, that land was now part of the Persian Empire. They were still under foreign rule, and the promised Davidic king was nowhere to be found. They answered to Persia, paid taxes to Persia, and lived with the constant reminder that Persia ruled the world. "We are slaves today," cried the returned exiles, "slaves in the land you gave our ancestors" (Neh. 9:36).

Some returnees lost hope that God would ever restore them, so they ended up conforming to the Persian way of life. Many of the men, even the religious leaders, married pagan women, disregarded the Sabbath, and neglected temple worship (Ezra 9–10; Neh. 13). Instead of being a holy nation and kingdom of priests, they simply lived like the nations around them. There was, however, a faithful remnant who followed the steady leadership of Ezra, Nehemiah, Zerubbabel, and other Jews who worked to maintain their distinct identity as a holy nation, even while being exiles in their own land.

> To live in exile, then, is to embody a
> posture of submissive resistance.

The exile didn't truly end when Persia allowed the Jews to return home, and this notion of still being in exile was a common theme in Jewish writing between the Testaments.[31] Greece would conquer Persia, and Rome would conquer Greece. Through it all, Israel's exilic sociopolitical identity, forged in the crucible of Babylon, continued to shape how followers of God viewed themselves in the shadow of empire. It was natural for the Jewish writers of the New Testament to refer to Jesus' followers as "exiles" and to Rome as the new Babylon.[32] These explicit references to exile in the New Testament draw on a deep well of Jewish thought, as Daniel Smith-Christopher says: "The entire New Testament is written from the perspective of exile."[33]

To live in exile, then, is to embody a posture of submissive resistance. The reason exiles don't take up arms in revolt against Babylon isn't because they think highly of Babylon. It's that they put their hope in God. Submission is fueled by hope: hope that Babylon's reign is temporary, that God's reign is ultimate and eternal, and that in a short while God will destroy Babylon. Yet this hope doesn't mean indifference to or passivity in the face of evil. On the contrary, exilic hope results in resistance as well as submission. Faithfulness in exile is "nonconformity to the world *as the basis from which to work for change*."[34] Exiles testify to the world that they are citizens of a kingdom whose King is a slain Lamb.

Jewish Responses to Empire

Living in the shadow of empire provoked various responses among the Jewish people. Some became *syncretists* who blended the empire's values with their Jewish faith. Leaders married pagan women and embraced imperial goals of power and domination. Herod the Great is one extreme example. Ethnically, he was part Jewish and engaged in some Jewish practices. He also renovated the Jerusalem temple, making it one of the wonders of the ancient world. But Herod was drunk with Roman power and violence. He ruled with a heavy hand, murdered people who threatened his rule, and lived a life of luxury and indulgence. He mirrored the ways of Rome and looked nothing like a Deuteronomy 17 king. Herod was like an ancient version of a modern-day politician, using religion to consolidate power but ruling in ways indistinguishable from those of other secular leaders.

In addition to the syncretists, there were the *separatists*, such as the Jewish sect known as the Essenes. These Jews all but removed themselves from society, forming countercultural communities of purity and holiness. Some even fled to the desert by the Dead Sea to form a separatist movement. They caught a glimpse of the nonconformist vision of living in exile, but they neglected the original mission of God's people to be a kingdom of priests. Instead of trying to be a light to the nations, these separatists hunkered down to await the day when God would return and destroy the pagan nations and wayward Jews.

Then there were the *revolutionaries*. They too understood that they were exiles, but they didn't want to remain in exile. Rather, they sought to overthrow their Gentile rulers through violent insurrection and establish God's kingdom on earth. Some enjoyed a brief period of success, like the Maccabean family, who revolted against their Greek overlords and enjoyed autonomous rule in the land of Israel for eighty years or so (142–63 BC). After power and wealth got to their heads, however, their mini-kingdom began to crumble. In 63 BC, the mighty Roman nation crushed the flickering resistance and reestablished Gentile rule over the land of Israel. The earlier Maccabean success wouldn't be forgotten, however. The seeds of revolt were planted, and for the next 150 years, many messianic revolutionaries would spring up and try to establish the empire of God by force.[35] In the New Testament, the Zealots and the sicarii ("dagger men") were bearers of the revolutionary tradition.

The Pharisees were a somewhat diverse group of Jews who reflected both separatist and revolutionary tendencies. The very term *Pharisee* comes from the Hebrew *parash*, which means "to separate." But the Pharisees didn't go as far as the Essenes and escape to the desert. They negotiated their purity while living a relatively normal civic life. Some Pharisees were open to revolution, and we know of several historical instances where a Pharisee participated in insurrection against Rome.[36]

Notice what all these responses had in common, a trait we've discussed earlier: they saw religion and politics as inseparable. Religious identity shaped a person's political practices and beliefs.

The *syncretists* believed that worshipping Yahweh was perfectly compatible with giving their allegiance to whatever new Babylon was ruling the world. The *separatists* established alternative civic communities detached from society, and they did this because of their religious views. The *revolutionaries* sought to establish God's empire on earth to replace the Roman Empire.

Jesus was born into a world bursting with various perspectives about the kingdom of Rome and its relation to the kingdom of God. Jesus could very well have followed one of the popular responses to Rome, but he didn't. He didn't wave the Roman flag alongside the Jewish one or escape to the desert to await the kingdom of God, nor did he join the revolutionaries in violent insurrection. Jesus also didn't go around preaching about a nonpolitical kingdom, one that is spiritual, not material, where God's kingdom exists in your heart with no relation to the creation that's destined to burn.

As we'll explore in the next chapter, Jesus' kingdom didn't fit neatly into any of the available categories of his day. Indeed, Jesus subverted the ways of the Roman Empire from his birth to his death. Resistance was woven into the sermons he preached, the language he used, and the actions he performed. He confronted Rome even while submitting to it. His kingdom wasn't a mere spiritual abstraction, but it also wasn't revolutionary and violent. His reign carried on Israel's original mission to be a kingdom of priests that would turn the world upside down. Jesus would nonviolently "crush all those kingdoms" (Dan. 2:44) *by* being crushed by the kingdom of Rome. And his submissive resistance would literally cost him his life.

Chapter 4

JESUS, THE NEW ISRAEL, AND THE KINGDOM NOT OF THIS WORLD

Rome never crucified religious leaders for preaching religious messages. They crucified political insurrectionists for treason.

The Roman cross was the ultimate piece of propaganda. It was designed to inflict unbearable pain and, even more importantly, to dishonor criminals and anyone associated with them. Rome crucified many Jews around the time of Jesus. All of them were guilty of insurrection, and some of them had been hailed as messiahs prior to their death. Crucifixion acted as a deterrent—persuading other aspiring insurrectionists to reconsider their vocation.

The crucifixion of Jesus bears tremendous theological meaning. It's how God atoned for the sins of his people. The cross also bears political meaning. It reveals how Jesus' mission and message were interpreted in the first century. Jesus wasn't crucified for preaching a spiritual gospel about the forgiveness of sins and eternal life. Rome couldn't care less about a religion that focused merely on people's private spirituality. Rome was actually very tolerant of other religions, as long as people maintained their patriotism toward the empire. The only religions that raised concern were those that destabilized society or posed a threat to Roman rule. What Rome wouldn't tolerate was insubordination. Jesus was crucified because he was perceived to be subverting the empire, and, as we'll see, Rome's perception was largely accurate.

When I say "largely accurate," I'm not suggesting that this perception was *absolutely* accurate. Jesus made clear that he wasn't a revolutionary seeking to violently overthrow Rome, as many would-be messiahs had attempted before him. But it's equally clear that he wasn't an apolitical preacher of spiritual truths who started a religion that could exist alongside allegiance to Rome. Jesus wasn't leading a revolt, at least not a violent one. But he was establishing a tangible empire on earth, which confronted and subverted imperial oppression and domination. Jesus came to establish God's kingdom on earth.

The Kingdom of God

Kingdom is a word that's often lost on modern ears. When I hear *kingdom*, I mostly think of medieval knights, damsels in distress, and *Monty Python and the Holy Grail*. When we read the word *kingdom* in the Bible, we often understand it as simply a spiritual word, a reference to salvation, Christ's reign in our hearts, or some future existence somewhere up in heaven. But as we saw in the book of Daniel, *kingdom* is profoundly political. It's the same word used to refer to the empires of Babylon, Persia, Greece, and Rome. The Greek word for "kingdom," *basileia*, was widely used to refer to the Roman Empire. It was also used by Jewish revolutionaries like the Maccabees, who tried to establish God's kingdom through violent insurrection. Jesus didn't do away with the political connotations of *kingdom*—if he'd intended this, he probably would have used a different word. Rather, Jesus sought to retain the political nature of *kingdom* while gutting the term of its arrogant associations with people seeking to rule the world through power, violence, and coercion.

In the vocabulary of Jesus, *kingdom* "denotes a geopolitical reality" and refers to "the *redeemed community under Jesus*."[1] When he went around preaching about "the kingdom of God," he was talking about the continuation of God's original mission to Israel: to be a kingdom of priests and a light to the nations. This mission has been refracted through exile, where God's people are stripped of political power and national identity. This kingdom of priests embodies God's reign on earth not by forming an allegiance to one particular nation but by wandering as exiles among the nations. The upside-down nature of this kingdom continues on.

The concept of the kingdom of God is the main content of Jesus' life and teaching. Not only does the word *basileia* occur more than a hundred times in the Gospels, but even where the word doesn't occur, the concept does. Jesus was repeatedly referred to as the Son of David, the Messiah, and the Son of Man—and all these titles are unintelligible apart from the concept of kingdom. The kingdom where this Messiah reigns is not just any kingdom but the upside-down kingdom we read about in the Old Testament, with a Deuteronomy 17 king at its head and a nonconforming people for citizens. To reconstitute this kingdom, the King would need to deliver a new constitution.

The Sermon on the Mount

The gospel writers often described Jesus in a way reminiscent of significant scenes in the Old Testament. For instance, Luke famously correlates the story of Mary, Jesus' mother, with Hannah, Samuel's mother. Both mothers experienced an unlikely birth of a child who would be a significant leader, and both sang songs of praise that use the same lyrics.[2] The early chapters of Matthew likewise exhibit one of the most in-your-face correlations between the story of Israel and the life of Christ. Matthew framed Jesus as a kind of new Moses who was constituting a new Israel to embody an upside-down kingdom.[3] Both Moses and Jesus were born in the midst of the slaughtering of infants by a tyrant king (Ex. 1:8–22; Matt. 2:16–21). Both were called from Egypt to deliver their people (Ex. 2–3; Matt. 2:13–15). Both passed through water (Ex. 14; Matt. 3:13–17). Both endured forty years/days of wilderness testing (Num. 14:26–35; Matt. 4:1–11). And both delivered a law from a mountain (Ex. 20–24; Matt. 5–7) to twelve tribes/disciples. To make the connection especially clear, Matthew's phrasing "he went up on the mountain" (5:1 CSB) occurs verbatim in three places in the Old Testament—all of which refer to Moses going up on Sinai to receive the law (Ex. 19:3; 24:18; 34:4 in the Septuagint).

Matthew, then, wanted us to understand Jesus as a kind of New Moses delivering a New Law to a New Israel. This New Law (the Sermon on the Mount) isn't completely new; it's rooted in the same law God gave Moses on Sinai. But it's not a mere replication of Sinai. Rather, Jesus took the same principles that shaped the law of Moses into a countercultural constitution and radicalized them even further.

Imagine the revolutionary excitement in the air as this alleged Messiah sat down with his twelve disciples on a mountainside in the style of Moses—the same Moses who delivered Israel's twelve tribes from the oppressive Egyptian Empire. Jesus had been gathering followers and preaching "the good news of the kingdom" (Matt. 4:23). Now he was telling his followers what this kingdom would look like. But instead of giving instructions on how to overthrow Rome—the new Egypt—he told them that true power is expressed in what the world sees as weakness and defeat.

"Blessed are the poor in spirit," "the meek," "the merciful," "the peacemakers," and even "those who are persecuted because of righteousness" (5:3–10). Kingdom citizens will look very little like citizens of the conquering kingdoms of this world. "In the beatitudes, Jesus has the disciples imagine a different world, a different identity for themselves, a different set of practices, a different relationship to the status quo," writes Warren Carter. In this way, citizens of the upside-down kingdom "begin to counter patterns imbibed from the culture of the imperial world."[4]

Jesus' new constitution for his kingdom people is filled with radically countercultural ways of living. We don't just refrain from murder but abstain from anger (5:21–26). We prohibit not just adultery but even lust (5:27–30). We avoid divorce (5:31–32) and tell the truth (5:33–37). We don't seek vengeance but turn the other cheek (5:38–42). And contrary to the values of every empire on earth, we don't just love our neighbors; we even love our enemies (5:43–48). We forgive those who sin against us (6:12–15), smash the idolatry of wealth (6:19–24), and put our hope in God rather than the endless quest for comfort and security (6:25–34). Though our light may shine for others to see (5:14–16), we don't virtue signal to gain honor in the eyes of others (6:1–4). We shun hypocrisy (7:1–5), expose falsehood (7:15–20), and trust the Father, who loves to give good gifts to his children (7:7–12).

Far from being a checklist for private spiritual living, the Sermon on the Mount is both personal and political—it's the new constitution for the coming kingdom that Daniel prophesied about, the one that will crush the kingdoms of this world (2:44). In the words of Jonathan Sgalambro, "The kingdom of heaven is on a collision course with the kingdoms and powers of this world, and we are 'blessed' to go along for the ride."[5] As the new and better Moses, Jesus sought to create a new society, an alternative *polis*, a new Israel that's designed, like historic Israel, to be unlike the surrounding nations.

Jesus' new constitution for his kingdom people is filled with radically countercultural ways of living.

Throughout Jesus' life and ministry, we see him explaining what this kingdom would look like. His holistic kingdom ethic includes personal morality: he showed us how to pray, instructed us not to lust, and invited us not to be anxious about our daily needs (Luke 12:22–34). But these themes of personal holiness are intertwined with the larger fabric of a sociopolitical ethic. He outlined how the church, as a political community, is to live faithfully in God's creation.

For instance, Jesus echoed many of Israel's economic principles: Resources are shared, generosity is praised, and the abuse of wealth is viciously condemned. Social hierarchies are deconstructed as the poor are elevated, women are humanized, and those in positions of power are considered no better than household servants. Foreigners and immigrants are welcomed, enemies are loved, and barriers to ethnic reconciliation are torn down. Jesus' life and teaching established a counterintuitive rhythm of nonviolence and nonretaliation. He promoted a countercultural sexual ethic that elevates singleness, welcomes the eunuch, and holds marriage in high esteem without idolizing it.

Jesus wasn't just forming a church filled with individuals striving to live lives of individual holiness. Rather, he was building an *ekklēsia* that embodied a sociopolitical ethic reminiscent of Israel's "not like the nations" way of life. This *basileia* ("kingdom") wasn't a metaphor for personal salvation, nor was it some place where people hope to go when they die, nor was it simply the spiritual reign of God in the here and now, before its physical manifestation when Jesus returns.[6] Jesus' announcement of God's kingdom was very much political, inasmuch as politics "involves the proper ordering of social practices and relationships, and patterns of economic exchange within a social group."[7]

Jesus declared that God's kingdom was breaking into human history in real, physical, tangible ways. The problem is, the first century already had one of those. Any announcement of another kingdom would have been viewed as a threat to Rome's political reign. No one knew this better than the Roman governor Pilate.

The King and His Kingdom

Jesus' conversation with Pilate in John 18–19 is highly relevant for our topic, since the political nature of concepts like king and kingdom is unmistakable. Pilate asked Jesus, "Are you the king of the Jews?" (18:33), and Jesus answered the question with his own question: "Is that your own idea … or did others talk to you about me?" (v. 34). Jesus didn't deny that he's a king, but he wanted to define kingship on his own terms: "My kingdom is not of this world. If it were, my servants would fight to prevent my arrest by the Jewish leaders. But now my kingdom is from another place" (v. 36).

Again, Jesus wasn't referring to some nonpolitical, nonmaterial reign of God "in your heart" and nowhere else. His point wasn't to deny that he's a real king over a material kingdom. Rather, he was defining what kind of kingdom he was establishing.

Pilate's response confirms that Jesus was claiming to be a king: "You are a king, then!" (v. 37). If he had understood Jesus to be preaching a spiritual, apolitical kingdom, he wouldn't have batted an eye. Rome didn't crucify people for telling others to accept some

Jewish god into their hearts. They crucified people suspected to be a threat to their empire.

Pilate's conversation with the Jewish leaders drives the point home. They told him, "If you let this man go, you are no friend of Caesar. *Anyone who claims to be a king opposes Caesar*" and "We have no king but Caesar" (19:12, 15). Pilate was hesitant to crucify Jesus until this point. But once he felt that Jesus' kingship was in opposition to Caesar's, he had the legal grounds for crucifixion. This is why he posted a placard on the cross that read "The king of the Jews" (Mark 15:26; cf. Matt. 27:37; Luke 23:38). Pilate had no warrant to crucify a mere religious teacher. But he had a duty to crucify any self-proclaimed king who posed a threat to the Roman imperial order.

When Jesus said that his kingdom was "not of this world," then, he "does not mean that his kingdom has nothing to do with politics or worldly matters."[8] After all, Jesus' kingdom brought healing to the sick, food for the hungry, justice for the oppressed, radical welcome to the outsider, dignity to women, a sexual and marriage ethic rooted in the Creator's design, a ruthless challenge to the wealthy and elite, and a whole host of other material matters. All these things were "political"—and, if you were Roman, "politically subversive."[9]

Kingdom *Polis*

Jesus was a real king establishing a tangible kingdom on earth, one that was intended not to overthrow the Roman Empire but to exist within it, embodying "God's reign as an alternative to the empire's societal reality."[10]

As outposts of this kingdom, then, the church is like mini *polises* dotted throughout the world as expressions of God's global empire. Instead of thinking of theology and social ethics as an incongruent binary—theology belongs inside the church while social ethics are outside the church—the church should be the kind of society we hope to see in the world.

We should become the Sermon on the Mount and the kingdom not of this world.

But what exactly does this look like? We've got a lot more biblical ground to cover, and I'm holding off on diving too deep into application before the foundation has been sufficiently laid. However, I can't help but think of a small concrete example of what it means to live as a political *polis* in the midst of the political culture wars that surround us.

America's health care system is one of many hotly debated political topics, and people's viewpoints are often rooted in partisan camps. Many on the left want free universal health care, while many on the right say this would cripple the economy and lower the quality of care. And so the debate rages on. Rather than getting wrapped up in Babylon's political debates, one large church in Missouri called The Crossing looked to Jesus to see if his kingdom ethic has anything to say about the matter. They noticed that, in Jesus' first sermon, he declared that the Spirit "has anointed me to proclaim good news to the poor ... to set the oppressed free, to proclaim the year of the Lord's favor" (Luke 4:18–19). "The year of the Lord's favor" refers back to the Year of Jubilee (Lev. 25)—that radical economic law where, every fifty years, financial debts would be forgiven. So they decided to do that. To do what Jesus said. To be the kind of *polis* we want to see in the world.

The Crossing teamed up with a nonprofit called RIP Medical Debt to help forgive $43 million of medical debt across the state of Missouri. "As crazy as it sounds," says the church, "something like this happened every fifty years in ancient Israel. It was called the Jubilee. A day of liberation. Debts forgiven. Indentured servants released. Mortgaged property returned. And on this same day everyone's sins were forgiven—even spiritual debts get paid off."[11]

We should become the Sermon on the Mount and the kingdom not of this world.

The church's embrace of Jesus' upside-down kingdom ethic not only affected their own people with debt but also spilled over into thirty-one counties in the state.[12] "If anyone asks why we wanted to do this, the answer is very simple. Jesus did it for us. Now he's freed us to do it for others."[13]

This reminds me of what the pagan emperor Julian (fourth century AD) said of the early church: "[They] support not only their own poor but ours as well."[14] To reach the world, we need to first *be* the church, to witness to "the world with a political alternative the world would not otherwise know."[15] This doesn't mean the church shouldn't care at all about national politics and health care policies. There might be a place for, say, helping reform the country's health care system (whatever that may look like).

We just don't make these things ultimate. We don't put our primary hope in Babylon to embody the kind of kingdom God intends, when we—the global church—have the resources and power to live out Christ's upside-down kingdom values.

Chapter 5

JESUS AND THE SUBVERSION OF EMPIRE

Jesus furnished his small band of disciples, his "new Israel," with a new constitution, which carried many sociopolitical ramifications. And as we saw from Jesus' interaction with Pilate, Rome raised an eyebrow—and a cross—at all this talk of king and kingdom. But Jesus' crucifixion isn't the only time we see the political nature of the gospel laid bare. There are many instances in Christ's ministry where he subtly—or not so subtly—subverted the values of the Roman Empire.

It's easy for modern readers to miss this dynamic, especially those of us who are quite fond of the empire we're living in. What I want to do in this chapter is take us back to the first century and try to understand how a first-century reader would have perceived the life and mission of Jesus. My goal is quite narrow. I'm not trying to create a comprehensive political theology or make applications that go beyond the point of the text. I simply want to show that Jesus was subversively critical of empire, which in his day was ruled from Rome. Jesus wasn't politically neutral. He also didn't have a favorite Roman ruler or encourage his followers to take sides in Rome's political arguments. Rather, Jesus was well aware that his message about the coming of God's kingdom carried political connotations that would make Rome deeply suspicious of his intent.[1]

We could look at dozens of scenes in the Gospels, but for the sake of space, we'll consider just eight events that, when read from a first-century perspective, sent subversive signals to the political authorities.

1. The Politics of Christ's Birth

The birth of Christ is framed as a politically significant event. In Matthew's account, the magi visited Jerusalem and asked King Herod—who was ethnically part Jewish but politically 100 percent Roman—about someone born "king of the Jews" (2:2). Herod was greatly disturbed and rightly so: "king of the Jews" was the political title that Rome had given *him*.[2] There was room for only one king of the Jews. Herod naturally suspected an insurrection, which is why he slaughtered the children of Bethlehem. It wasn't the first time he had killed people who posed a threat to his political power.[3]

Joseph and Mary took Jesus, escaped to Egypt, and returned after Herod died. Matthew tells us that this was to fulfill the words of the prophet Hosea: "Out of Egypt I called my son" (2:15; cf. Hos. 11:1). Hosea's words refer to Israel's exodus from Egypt; "my son" is the enslaved nation, and "Egypt" is the oppressive empire that enslaved them and made a botched attempt to slaughter their numerous children (Ex. 1).

The way Matthew retold the birth of Christ deliberately alludes to God's deliverance of his oppressed people through the exodus. As we saw previously, Matthew described Jesus as the new Moses who would lead his people out of the Egyptian Empire, which made Herod (the puppet king of Rome) the new pharaoh and face of the imperial regime. In the book of Exodus, God's rule didn't exist peacefully alongside Pharaoh's reign. The two were in competition. By mapping the birth of King Jesus onto the events of the exodus, Matthew's account whispers a dangerous message: the true King has arrived, a new exodus is underway, and earthly rulers are on their way out.

Luke also recounted Christ's birth, and his language is even more political than Matthew's. Luke mentioned two Roman rulers, Caesar Augustus and the governor Quirinius, and set Christ's birth against the backdrop of Rome's call for a census (2:1–2). The purpose of the census was to determine taxation, and to first-century ears, taxation was a form of political oppression. Taxation back then was different from how it's done in democratic countries today. About 1 percent of the population held almost all the wealth and power, while almost everyone else lived in what would be considered poverty by most modern standards.[4] By and large, taxes funded the extravagant lifestyle of the elite and Rome's glamorous architecture, which showed off the empire's glory and power. Taxation was a symbol of subjugation; it reminded people who was dominant and who was being dominated.[5] In fact, just a decade after Jesus was born, a revolutionary named Judas (not Iscariot) started an insurrection against Rome because they had forced another census on the Jewish people for the purpose of taxation.[6] The political leader who initiated the census that sparked this rebellion was Quirinius—the same

Quirinius mentioned in Luke 2. By naming this politician, Luke was activating the agitated political memories of his readers.

Luke tells us that Joseph and Mary went "to Bethlehem the town of David, because he belonged to the house and line of David" (v. 4). Mentioning David here also kicked up political dust. The Lord had promised the son of David: "I will make the nations your inheritance, the ends of the earth your possession" (Ps. 2:8). The psalmist added, "Therefore, you kings, be wise; be warned, you rulers of the earth" (v. 10). After Jesus was born, the angels told the shepherds, "A Savior has been born to you; he is the Messiah, the Lord" (Luke 2:11). Christians today are used to thinking of titles like "Savior" and "Lord" as purely spiritual or religious titles. But in the first century, these titles were widely used to describe the Roman emperor. As we'll see in the next chapter, they carried profound political implications. The way Luke described Jesus' birth narrative, then, constitutes "an ideological clash with the saviour of the Christians and that of the citizens of Rome."[7]

I'm not suggesting that we should ignore the profoundly spiritual significance of these birth narratives, which certainly exceeds their political implications. But I also want us to recognize the clear political connotations the biblical writers were expressing—connotations that would have been heard loud and clear by any first-century reader steeped in Roman propaganda.

2. The Baptism of the New Emperor

Two pieces of Christ's baptism have political overtones. First, the Father's voice said, "You are my Son, whom I love; with you I am well pleased"—an allusion to Psalm 2:7 and Isaiah 42:1. Second, the Spirit descended on Jesus "in bodily form like a dove" (Luke 3:22).

Both Psalm 2 and Isaiah 42 describe the Messiah in relation to the nations. Isaiah said he "will bring justice to the nations" (42:1), while the psalmist said he "will break" the nations "with a rod of iron" and "dash them to pieces like pottery" (2:9). However we understand these statements, it's certain that Jesus was neither politically neutral nor nationalistic. He sought neither to violently overthrow Rome nor to conform to Roman ways. But in some way, his reign would be in opposition to the empire.

The mention of the Spirit descending "like a dove" has spawned many explanations. Ancient writers often described the rise of Roman emperors by using bird imagery—specifically, the image of an eagle. New Testament scholar Patrick Schreiner points out, "Eagles symbolized power and authority, establishing a candidate's claim to the throne. Because the eagle had a distinctive relationship with Jupiter, it became the emblem of the Roman Empire." Doves, on the other hand, "symbolize peace, purity, serenity, and gentleness."[8] Schreiner therefore suggests that "the dove confirms the political nature of Jesus' message and ministry, yet it also indicates Jesus' political program was radically different from Rome's. He was establishing a different kind of kingdom."[9]

3. The Temptation of Christ and the Political Authority of Satan

Matthew, Mark, and Luke all mention Jesus' temptation by Satan in the wilderness. Matthew and Luke record three specific temptations, one of which is Satan's offer to give Jesus "all the kingdoms of the world and their splendor" if only Jesus would worship him (Matt. 4:8).

Some readers might assume that the offer wasn't genuine, since Satan doesn't have authority over "all the kingdoms of the world." But why would we assume this? Jesus doesn't seem to have thought Satan was lying about his authority; otherwise, he probably would have said so. Plus, satanic authority over worldly kingdoms is a steady theme throughout Scripture. Daniel, John, and Paul all talk about the nations being under the control of Satan.[10] First-century readers familiar with Scripture would have readily assumed that the offer was real.

Jesus' ongoing battles against Satan and demonic forces were certainly spiritual. His rejection of Satan's offer shows that Jesus' allegiance was to his Father alone. Indeed, he would gain authority over the nations through a cross, not a sword. But this particular temptation also reveals how satanic forces are intertwined with the political authority of empires. As we'll discuss later, the book of Revelation says that Satan and Rome (and empires in general) are practically joined at the hip (Rev. 12–13). Throughout Scripture, we see a blurry line between Jesus' war against Satan and against the empires under his sway, putting into question the modern attempt to oppose Satan while giving allegiance to the empire.

4. On Pigs and Politics

The healing of the demon-possessed man in Mark 5 is notoriously strange, and many commentators have tried to make sense of it. Jesus cast a bunch of demons out of a man after they asked for permission to possess a herd of pigs. Jesus granted their request, and the demons caused the pigs to rush headlong into the Sea of Galilee. The man got saved, but the pig farmers were understandably outraged. Jews, of course, neither ate nor herded pigs, so the story is set in Gentile territory. When Jesus asked for the name of the demon, the answer was telling: "My name is Legion" (v. 9).

What does any of this have to do with politics? While a bit subtler than other events, some elements in the story suggest a symbolic attack on Rome.

Legion is a term used to describe "the central unit of Rome's military."[11] In the first century, Rome's military was made up of approximately twenty-five legions, each possessing about six thousand troops.[12] These legions were spread throughout the empire, standing ready in case an insurrection broke out. And it just so happens that the tenth Roman legion, which was stationed in Palestine, had an animal mascot plastered on their shields and banners. It was a pig.[13]

When Roman legions weren't fighting, their mere presence was a powerful sign of who was in control, who could crush you should you get out of line. Since the Jews were a particularly feisty people, Roman troops were omnipresent throughout the land. The Gentile territory where the story is set would have been home turf for the military.

The reference to "legion" in Gentile territory where pigs were being herded—and quickly destroyed—seems to allude to the inbreaking of Christ's kingdom over Rome's military power. Part of Christ's mission was to dethrone Satan and destroy his demonic army. Since Satan's forces were so tethered to Rome's empire, any victory against Satan would also throw shade on the source of Rome's power.

That seems to be at least part of the point of Mark 5. By casting Christ's victory over demonic forces in political language, Mark signaled to his Roman audience that the kingdom of God couldn't be stopped by Rome's silly military.

5. Subverting the Empire by Washing Feet

The radicality of Jesus' foot-washing incident can hardly be overstated (John 13:1–20). For a king to wash his disciples' feet wasn't just some random humble gesture on the part of Christ. It was a bold attempt at turning Rome's view of power and authority upside down.

John set up the story by alerting us to Satan's power at work in Judas, who was about to betray Jesus (v. 2). John then tells us that "the Father had put all things under [Jesus'] power" (v. 3), so we would expect Jesus to conquer both Satan and Judas. And he did—sort of. He overcame evil *not* by raising a sword but by stripping down to his loincloth, taking "the form of a slave" (Phil. 2:7 NRSVUE), in order to establish a new political order that was critical of Rome's values of status and hierarchy.

Roman society, like most other ancient societies, was an honor/shame culture based on social hierarchy. And members of the empire were obsessed with public reputation; it was a fundamental Roman value. One example of this is the *cursus honorum*, or "race for honors,"[14] where various civic offices carried with them different levels of status and honor. People of all social classes sought to attain whatever level of office was within reach, and their motivation was quite simply public recognition. "Public honor—not public service—was central to office-holding in the Roman world."[15]

The quest for various offices—along with their honorable titles—was common among the highest elites. The emperor, of course, held the most honorable title, and after him, members of the Senate. But this "race for honors" wasn't just reserved for the highest tip of the social pyramid. It penetrated all levels of social classes—imperial elites, local elites, and everyone else who was part of the masses. Accumulating titles of honor that elevated one's social status permeated the lives of most people in the Roman world.

Jesus' life and ministry constantly confronted social hierarchies that were embedded in the Roman way of life. Prior to his birth, Mary and Elizabeth were lifted up in high esteem as they testified to the coming of the Messiah (Luke 1:26–80). Mary's Magnificat is all about the theme of reversal, where God has "looked with favor on the humble condition of His slave," "scattered the proud," "toppled the mighty from their thrones and exalted the lowly," and "satisfied the hungry with good things and sent the rich away empty" (vv. 48, 51–53 HCSB). News of Jesus' birth first went not to people in high places but to lowly shepherds out in the field (2:8–20). And it was women, who held less social status than men, who were the first witnesses to Christ's resurrection.[16]

Jesus frequently deconstructed social hierarchies, where people at the top held more honor than people at the bottom: "Many who are first will be last, and the last first."[17] "Whoever exalts himself shall be humbled, and whoever humbles himself shall be exalted."[18] When the disciples were arguing over who would be greatest in the kingdom, Jesus turned the whole paradigm of leadership and authority on its head:

> Jesus called them to Himself and said, "You know that the rulers of the Gentiles domineer over them, and those in high position exercise authority over them. It is not this way among you, but whoever wants to become prominent among you shall be your servant [*diakonos*], and whoever desires to be first among you shall be your slave [*doulos*]; just as the Son of Man did not come to be served, but to serve, and to give His life as a ransom for many." (Matt. 20:25–28 NASB; cf. Luke 22:25–27)

Status and power in God's kingdom will look nothing like they do in the kingdoms of this world. It's not that Christian leaders should be weak and passive. It's that true strength and power come through sacrifice and service.

6. Paying Taxes as Political Resistance

We come now to Jesus' famous "render unto Caesar" moment, recorded in three of the four gospels.[19] The Pharisees and Herodians tried to catch Jesus in his words by asking him whether it was right to pay taxes to Caesar. Jesus responded by requesting to see a coin and then asking, "Whose image is this? And whose inscription?" They replied, "Caesar's," to which Jesus responded, "Give back to Caesar what is Caesar's and to God what is God's'" (Mark 12:13–17).

This scene appears to support a kind of "God and country" ideology, where allegiance to Caesar can coexist alongside one's allegiance to God. But there are several reasons I don't think this is how the first-century readers would have understood it.[20]

First, Jesus' response confounded both the Pharisees and the Herodians. The Herodians were a pro-Roman Jewish faction, while the Pharisees were much more anti-Roman, even to the point of insurrection.[21] Had Jesus given a pro-Roman response, he would have satisfied the Herodians and angered the Pharisees. Had he advocated for not paying taxes, he might have pleased the Pharisees and provoked the Herodians. To refuse to pay taxes would have been a flagrant act of rebellion against Rome, planting the seeds of a violent revolution. But Jesus' response didn't fit within either ideology; it was neither patriotic nor revolutionary, since neither the Pharisees nor the Herodians were satisfied with it. Just as Jesus doesn't fit into the modern right/left binary, he didn't fit easily into the ancient pro-Rome/anti-Rome binary.

Second, taxation was a form of imperial oppression. As much as those of us in Western democratic countries might grumble when we pay taxes, our taxation is much different from Rome's. Scholars like Richard Bauckham explain that "taxation in the ancient world could not normally be perceived by the ordinary people who bore the main burden of it as having anything to do with their benefit. Taxation benefited the rulers, not the ruled."[22] Some taxes might have helped fund public services, like the building of roads and bridges. But even these were designed to serve the interests of the elite.[23] Taxation was the means by which the rich and powerful maintained their luxurious lifestyle, and it "was required for the maintenance of the

Empire's military power and bureaucratic structure."[24] In Jesus' day, taxation was synonymous with powerful people exploiting the poor. Whatever Jesus meant by giving back to Caesar what belonged to him, he certainly wasn't supporting all the immorality and injustice represented by taxation. Something subtler was going on.

Submitting to the empire does not mean celebrating the empire.

Third, when Jesus asked whose image was on the coin, he was probably being more facetious than serious. He knew very well whose image was on the coin. Roman coins were a significant piece of propaganda, constantly reminding people who ruled the world. Caesar's image on the coin was a violation of Jewish law, and coins were often inscribed with divine titles accredited to Caesar, which were blasphemy.[25] It's almost as if Jesus shrugged his shoulders after looking at the image and said, *Huh, who knew? I guess this coin belongs to that guy in Rome, since it has his arrogant face and false claims of divinity all over it. Here, why don't you just give it back to him, then?* Jesus wasn't actually showing his support of Caesar or saying anything particularly pro-Rome.

Fourth, Jesus' response of "Give back to Caesar what is Caesar's and to God what is God's" was a direct attack on Roman ideology. To claim that some things belong to God *and not also to Caesar* would have been scandalous. Fundamental to Roman ideology was the belief that Roman imperial rule *was* a manifestation of the gods. Imperial rule *was* divine rule. But Jesus casually disagreed as he flipped Caesar's coin back at the empire. In essence, Jesus was saying, *Caesar can have his stupid coin back, since my Father is the true emperor of the earth.* But he was also submitting to oppressive Roman taxation, since he still advocated for paying taxes, so he couldn't be accused of starting a revolution. Neither the Pharisees nor the Herodians had an answer. Caesar would get his idolatrous coin back, and Yahweh would get the whole universe.

Rather than legitimizing some kind of dual allegiance to God and empire, this scene embodies the subversive submissiveness that earlier Jews learned by living as exiles in the shadow of empire. Submitting to the empire does not mean celebrating the empire. It just means that citizens of God's empire recognize an authority much higher and more powerful than the self-proclaimed rulers of the earth.

7. The Politics of Crucifixion

In addition to its fundamental roles in Christian theology and ethics—as our means of salvation and our model of nonretaliation, forgiveness, and self-giving sacrifice—the crucifixion of Christ was also a profoundly political event. The true King of the earth submitted to the capital punishment of the empire as a means of defeating that very empire.

From a Roman perspective, crucifixion was the ultimate symbol of Roman domination. It was "not simply an act of extreme violence but also a form of 'ritualized remembrance,' a dramatic reenactment of Rome's conquest of the world with pointed propaganda objectives."[26] Rome believed their gods created the empire to establish peace and order in the world. Anyone who threatened to destabilize this order should be publicly punished and humiliated to deter other would-be insurrectionists.

Although crucifixion inflicted extreme pain, its ultimate goal was public humiliation and denigration. "The violence of the cross went beyond physical punishment to symbolic annihilation; the destruction of the victim's flesh narrated Rome's capacity to suppress every threat to the state's entire sovereignty."[27] The cross was a violent form of Roman propaganda, a way to advertise the power of the empire. The first-century Roman author Quintilian stated plainly that "when we [Romans] crucify criminals the most frequented roads are chosen, where the greatest number of people can look and be seized by this fear."[28] Crucifixion was so horrific that Roman writers urged others not to talk about it. "The very word 'cross,'" wrote Cicero, "should be far removed not only from the person of a Roman citizen but from his thoughts, his eyes and his ears.... The mere mention of [it] is unworthy of a Roman citizen."[29]

When we come to the New Testament, then, we must read the stories of Christ's crucifixion through this political lens (alongside its theological and ethical lenses). It is a parody of Rome's "dramatic reenactment of [their] conquest of the world with pointed propaganda objectives."[30] Rome exerted worldly power by crucifying Christ; Christ unleashed divine power into the world by being crucified by Rome.

The gospel writers turned the cross from a symbol of Roman power into an ironic picture of King Jesus' victory over the world. John in particular drove this point home by lining his narrative with frequent reminders that the Roman leaders were simply following the script of God's sovereign plan. The various events of Calvary were happening "so that Scripture would be fulfilled."[31] Rome was like a pawn in a divine chess game; they couldn't *not* play their silly power games while they continued to exalt King Jesus by lifting up his cross. Rome's pseudo-authority had nothing to do with the real reason Christ was crucified. Jesus had been announcing it all along (John 10:18; 19:11). He even borrowed typical Roman military terminology—*nikaō*, "conquer, overcome"—to foretell his victory on the cross: "I have conquered [*nikaō*] the world" (16:33 CSB). And in his dying breath, he announced his royal victory: *tetelestai*—"It is finished" (19:30).

By taking Rome's most feared symbol of power and turning it on its head, the gospel writers daringly challenged the foundations of imperial rule. Rome tried to squash an insurrection but ended up coronating a new King, who received his upside-down empire from the Ancient of Days.

8. The Politics of Resurrection and Ascension

Resurrection wasn't a common theme surrounding the Roman emperors, so it doesn't appear that Jesus' resurrection or the way the gospel writers retold it was intended to subvert the claims of the Caesars.[32] The political significance of resurrection is witnessed, however, by the fact that crucifixion—the ultimate display of Roman power—was made impotent by the power of God. The alleged power of Rome, advertised through the crucifixion of anyone who threatened their rule, was completely turned on its head when Jesus walked out of the grave a king. Little did the Roman leaders know that they were enthroning Jesus by crucifying him, but the irony is made clear through resurrection.

The proclamation "Jesus is King" is a political statement and creates a new lens through which we view the politics of Babylon.

Christ's subsequent ascension taps directly into imperial propaganda (Luke 24:50–53; Acts 1:9–11). At games held in honor of Caesar Augustus, it was reported that a comet appeared. Augustus took this as a sign that his adoptive father, Julius Caesar, had ascended into heaven and been adopted as a son of god. An event like this was called an apotheosis—the posthumous deification of a person. Many later Caesars (and George Washington himself) were given the same honor. "By narrating Jesus's ascent into heaven, Luke asserts that Jesus is the true ascended Lord."[33]

Conclusion

Christ's empire comes with its own values, social structures, moral mandates, and King. When people tried to force Jesus into various allegiances—*Are you an Essene or a Sadducee? A Zealot or a Herodian? Pro-taxation or anti-taxation?*—he ducked their invitations to become part of their tribe. I think he'd do the same with our modern political tribes—*Are you left or right, liberal or conservative, Democrat or Republican?*

The proclamation "Jesus is King" is a political statement and creates a new lens through which we view the politics of Babylon. It's all too common for us moderns to *begin* with political categories and then hustle these back to Scripture to see which ones are most "biblical." But what often happens is that our values are already (sometimes unconsciously) shaped by Babylonian categories, nurtured by a steady drip of propaganda, and *then* we find verses to support our preconceived commitments. Left-wing Christians sometimes highlight Christ's liberation of the oppressed and heart for the poor and say, "See, Jesus is on the left!" Right-wing Christians sometimes respond by saying, "No, Jesus valued the lives of unborn children—Jesus is conservative."

The problem is that Jesus doesn't neatly fit into any one point along our modern political spectrum. His kingdom is not of this world, and neither are his kingdom values. As my friend Paul Anleitner once said, "It's checkers to chess. The board looks the same, but Jesus isn't playing the same game. But if all you've ever known is checkers, when Jesus makes a move that looks like it's within the rules of that game, people go, 'See! He's on our team!'"[34]

Instead of starting with the left/right categories of Rome (or Babylon or Panama or the United States or wherever), we need to start with the political vision of Christ. We need to cultivate the habit of letting Christ's kingdom and its ethic determine our political values, because Christ's kingdom—and our membership in it—*is* a political identity.

Chapter 6

PAUL AND THE COUNTER-IMPERIAL GOSPEL

Like all previous empires, Rome believed they were exceptional, and they wanted everyone to know it. They proclaimed it through festivals, shrines, temples, public inscriptions, literature, architecture, sporting events, and even coins—Roman exceptionalism permeated every part of society. After all, they believed the gods had commissioned Rome to rule the world.[1] With such divine blessing, it was only a matter of time before people started to worship not only the gods of Rome but also the leaders of Rome. This led to the formation of imperial cults: the veneration of the emperor as divine.[2]

Emperor worship wasn't always a thing in the Roman world. It was even discouraged in some parts of the empire early on. But by the time the Christian movement was underway, hardly any pocket of the empire was free from some kind of veneration of Caesar.[3] This doesn't mean Rome imposed emperor worship on its people, nor did people exclusively worship the emperor while ignoring other gods. Roman society was polytheistic and pagan. There was always room for another god on the shelf.

Worshipping the emperor wasn't just a private act that some people did in their hearts. It was woven into the fabric of civic life. "These new imperial cults," New Testament scholar Greg Carey points out, "became the ritual bonds that held imperial society together, from the highest level of the province and its constituent cities, where the temples and shrines adorned the city centers and grand festivals were staged, extending into the neighborhood, associational, and even family levels." And "since the imperial temples housed provincial assemblies, banks, and marketplaces, they integrated religious, economic, civic, social, and political functions."[4]

There's no way Christians could have dodged all forms of social pressure when they clung to their confession that Jesus, not Caesar, is the ultimate King. Remember, politics and religion were intertwined. Refusing to venerate Caesar wasn't just a religious decision. It was politically unpatriotic.[5] It would have been like sitting during the national anthem at a Texas rodeo. It's not illegal to do so. But the social backlash would be profound.

Nevertheless, instead of trying to de-politicize their claims or privatize their religion, the early Christians did the opposite. When they proclaimed Jesus as the one true King over all other kings—including Roman emperors—they deliberately used the same political vocabulary that was widely used in Roman imperial ideology. Once you steep yourself in this political vocabulary, you will never again read the New Testament apolitically.

Shared Political Vocabulary

Along with calling Jesus "King," early Christians also called him "the Son of God."[6] This was a title given to many of the Roman Caesars, including Augustus,[7] Tiberius,[8] and Caligula.[9] One of the most frequent titles used of Christ was "Lord" (*kyrios*). This term has deep Old Testament roots, referring as it often does to Yahweh, the God of Israel. But "lord" was also widely used of the emperor, especially Nero, who reigned from AD 54 to 68 when most of Paul's letters were written.[10] To publicly say that *Jesus* is Lord suggested that Nero was not. It was a politically audacious thing to say.

Many other seemingly religious terms carried strong political connotations. Evidence has been gathered from inscriptions, documents, coins, art, and architecture, where we see Caesar described as "god,"[11] "savior," "benefactor,"[12] "creator,"[13] "chief priest,"[14] and "father."[15] Some Caesars were even called "shepherd" or "good shepherd," protectors of the Roman "flock."[16] Christians sometimes took whole phrases used to venerate the emperor and applied them to Christ:

Emperor Claudius was called "savior of all mankind" (*tōn pantōn anthrōpōn sōtēra*)[17]

Christ was called "Savior of all mankind" (*sōtēr pantōn anthrōpōn*)[18]

Emperor Claudius was described as "god manifest" (*theon epiphanē*)[19]

Christ was described as "God was manifested in the flesh" (*theos ephanerōthē en sarki*)[20]

"Savior" and "god" and "shepherd" weren't just churchy terms. In the first century, these were political terms that carried massive implications for how you situated yourself in the political landscape of the empire. To question whether Caesar was the true emperor— or, more offensively, to suggest that a Jew who was crucified by the power of Rome was actually *the* Lord, *the* Savior, *the* Son of God[21]— was to question the very foundation of Roman exceptionalism. It could start a riot, as we'll see.

Christians went on to hijack other Roman political terms to describe the reign of Christ. One of the most daring was the word "gospel" (*euangelion*)—a term that was loaded with political connotations in the ancient world.

"Gospel" does have deep roots in the Greek translation of the Old Testament, where it was used to describe the good news that Israel's God is the true, sovereign King of the world and that he would intervene to save his exiles and judge the oppressive Babylonian Empire: "You who *bring good news* to Zion … who *bring good news* to Jerusalem," Isaiah announced to the exiles in Babylon. "'Here is your God!' See, the Sovereign LORD comes with power, and he rules with a mighty arm" (40:9–10).

But "gospel" wasn't just an Old Testament term. It was widely used to describe the rise of a new Caesar to the throne of the empire or to announce a recent military victory of Rome.[22]

The birth of Caesar Augustus was hailed in one inscription as "the birthday of our god" who "marked for the world the beginning of *good news* [*euangelion*] through his coming." In fact, the inscription goes on, "With his appearance, Caesar exceeded hopes of all those who anticipated *good tidings* [*euangelion*] before us."[23] This inscription was written in Greek and Latin, and portions of it have been found in highly visible places in five different ancient cities in Asia,[24] which means it was intended for public propaganda. The message was designed to reinforce an ideology of Roman imperialism in the heart and mind of everyone in the empire. It publicly proclaimed the gospel of Rome.

Even the term "faith" (Greek: *pistis*; Latin: *fides*) carried political connotations, especially when used in relation to other terms like "gospel" and "kingdom." We often think of faith as mental assent, or belief in things you can't see. But biblical *pistis* in its first-century context is better understood as connoting allegiance to a king or ruler.[25] When Mark, who was writing to a Roman audience, recalled Jesus "proclaiming the good news" that "the kingdom of God has come near" and urging everyone to "repent and believe [*pisteuō*] the good news" (1:14–15), he was inviting his readers to make a decision that would forever reshape their political identity.

> To believe the gospel of Jesus and announce it to others in the first century was a politically subversive act.

Yes, the gospel is profoundly theological. It's the means by which people get saved. But it also reconfigures our relationship to the empire by shifting our allegiance elsewhere.

In the first-century context, "gospel" was a public announcement about a king. When early Christians "shared the gospel," they weren't inviting Roman people to accept Jesus into their hearts as their private Lord and Savior. Instead, they were announcing the sovereign kingship of Christ, who was paradoxically enthroned by Pilate on a Roman cross. To believe the gospel of Jesus and announce it to others in the first century was a politically subversive act. The early church wouldn't have recognized "gospel preaching" that galvanized allegiance to one of Rome's political parties as having anything to do with the Christian gospel.

Because they used the same political language as Rome, early Christians lived under constant suspicion that they were being unpatriotic toward the empire. Christians today don't live in the same environment; there are many differences between Christians living under Roman rule and those living in whatever fill-in-the-blank nation you're in today. And yet, Christians of every era should appreciate the fact that the first-century gospel was designed to wrench people's allegiance away from worldly kings and kingdoms and throw it on the one true King—Jesus.

Christians should be skeptical of the idea that secular politics and Christian theological claims live in two separate spheres or that someone's allegiance to Christ can happily coexist alongside their allegiance to the state. The very nature of the gospel—the announcement that Jesus is Lord—contradicts the claims of the empire. As you can imagine, preaching a gospel with such daring language didn't always fare well in the public square.

Paul's Counter-Imperial Gospel in the Book of Acts

Throughout the book of Acts, Christians embody both subversion and submission, just like the Jewish exiles before them.[26] The early Christians were constantly stirring up trouble as they performed healings and announced the messiahship and resurrection of Christ. Early in Acts, the trouble came from the Jews, but in the latter half of the book, Paul and others traveled deep into the Roman Empire, where they kept stirring up trouble by announcing the good news that Jesus was the new king on the throne.

To get a picture of how the gospel was received in this Greco-Roman context, I want to look at two cities where Paul preached Christ: Philippi (16:11–40) and Thessalonica (17:1–9). In each case, we'll witness some concrete ways in which the gospel interacted with Roman politics.

Patriotism and Citizenship

Philippi was one of the most patriotic and militaristic cities in the Roman world. It was the location where Mark Antony and Octavian (later named Caesar Augustus) defeated Brutus and Cassius, the conspirators who had assassinated Julius Caesar. After that victory, Octavian made Philippi a Roman colony, a rare and significant honor, and a number of veteran soldiers settled there.[27] Philippi's pro-military presence "guaranteed that Rome's social and religious values would permeate the settlement in some rather exceptional ways."[28] Luke specifically highlighted the fact that Philippi was "a Roman colony" (Acts 16:12). Nowhere else in Acts did he describe a city this way, even though Paul visited at least eight other cities that were Roman colonies. As Joseph Hellerman explains, "Luke here underscored the Romanness of the settlement, in preparation for the charge brought against the missionaries in the verses to follow."[29]

Philippi wasn't just militaristic; it was profoundly patriotic. It's been estimated that 40 percent of its inhabitants were Roman citizens, including about 33 percent of the Christians in Philippi.[30] Being a Roman citizen wasn't like being an American citizen, where almost everyone living in America has access to becoming a citizen. Most people under the Roman Empire would never and *could* never gain the honorable status of Roman citizenship. It was a prestigious privilege that helped galvanize one's allegiance to Rome. And, as we'll see, this appears to have been problematic for the Philippian church, since Paul devoted a significant portion of his letter to the tension between Roman citizenship and citizenship in Christ.

Patriotism and militarism. These were the cultural foundations of Philippi. Today it might seem like a prime location to plant a modern American megachurch, but this environment posed a challenge for Paul and his counter-imperial gospel.

Paul's visit to Philippi was going fine until he cast a demon out of a slave girl being trafficked for profit. Naturally, her owners got upset. Realizing "their hope of profit was gone" (Acts 16:19 CSB), they dragged Paul and Silas before the authorities and accused them of "seriously disturbing our city" and "promoting customs that are not legal for us as Romans to adopt or practice" (vv. 20–21 CSB). Whatever specific "customs" the accusers had in mind, something in Paul and Silas's gospel preaching was perceived as un-Roman—so much so that the authorities arrested Paul and Silas and threw them into prison.

The clash between gospel and empire appears throughout Paul's letter to the Philippian church. Several years after Paul founded a church at Philippi, he got word of some issues they were wrestling with, so he penned a letter of encouragement and exhortation.

Philippians 1:27—3:21 is one literary unit, and it's bookended with language of citizenship. Paul opens with an exhortation to "*live out your citizenship* [*politeuomai*] in a manner worthy of the gospel of Christ" (1:27, my translation). Most translations don't use this language, but the Greek word *politeuomai* is the verb form of the noun *politeuma*, which means "citizenship"; both words are based on the noun *polis*, which means "city." The verb form *politeuomai* has to do with living out one's citizenship, one's loyalty to the *polis*. This is the only time the verb is used in the New Testament epistles, probably because no other city struggled with such celebratory passion over Roman citizenship. To reorient the Philippian believers' priorities, Paul told them to direct their focus to "the gospel of Christ"—the good news that *Jesus* is Lord, *not Caesar*. It's as if Paul were saying, *Don't think that your Roman citizenship gains you more status, more honor, more prestige in the empire of God. Slaves have as much status as you. Now stop obsessing over your trivial Roman status, and keep your eyes fixed on the good news: Jesus—a Jew crucified by the power of your beloved Roman kings—is the true King to whom you owe your allegiance.*

Paul would go on to give a radically reorienting picture of social status in Philippians 2:5–11. Jesus became human flesh and descended to the lowest rung on the Roman social ladder—"taking the form of a slave" (v. 7 NRSVUE)—as a pathway to being exalted by his Father. Jesus submitted and served and obeyed—all the things that Roman kings would never do. He grabbed Rome's ladder to social honor and snapped it over his knee. While Roman citizens were clamoring to scale the empire's social pyramid, Jesus flipped the whole thing upside down. To be a king is to be a servant. Jesus' humiliation in suffering was the manner in which he was coronated as the emperor of all creation.

Paul closes out this literary unit with the letter's other reference to citizenship: "Our citizenship is in heaven, and we eagerly wait for a Savior from there, the Lord Jesus Christ. He will transform the body of our humble condition into the likeness of his glorious body, by the power that enables him to subject everything to himself" (3:20–21 CSB). *Citizenship, Savior, Lord, power, subject*—this short passage is loaded with political terminology. Paul's point is clear: the Philippians' allegiance to King Jesus had to reshape how they viewed themselves in the Roman world. Early-church leaders like Clement of Alexandria (circa AD 150–215) taught that "to be mindful of heavenly citizenship was to live as an expatriate."[31] Citizens of Christ's kingdom live as if they are strangers and aliens in a foreign land—as exiles in the shadow of the empire.

Turning the World Upside Down

Luke tells us about a similar incident in Thessalonica. Paul went into the synagogue to preach Jesus as Messiah ("Anointed One, King"), and the Jews got upset. So they went out and "brought together some wicked men from the marketplace, formed a mob, and started a riot in the city" (Acts 17:5 CSB). Keep in mind that the Roman Empire was tolerant of most religions; they wouldn't have cared about what some Jew said in some synagogue somewhere—unless, of course, he was suspected of stirring up sedition or trying to start a revolution. The mob called a "public assembly" (*dēmos*) to determine what to do with Paul and his companions (v. 5 CSB). Their accusation? "These men who have turned the world upside down have come here too," the mob said. "They are all acting contrary to Caesar's decrees, saying that there is another king—Jesus" (vv. 6–7 CSB).

The Thessalonians were steeped in Roman imperial ideology. Caesar Claudius was the emperor at the time, and he had been declared "the most divine Caesar and truly our savior" (*tou theiotatou Kaisaros kai hōs alēthōs sōtēros hēmōn*), among other divine epithets that early Christians also used of Christ.[32] Coins minted earlier in Thessalonica show Julius Caesar wearing a crown and bearing the title *theos* ("god"), with the coins' other side showing an image of Augustus and the word "Thessalonica."[33] It's no wonder Paul's announcement about "another king" raised quite a stir.

Scholars have argued over what alleged "decrees" the Thessalonians thought Paul was opposing.[34] Whatever Luke had in mind, he clearly connected the issue to Paul's claim that "there is another king—Jesus." Paul and Silas stirred up trouble in

Thessalonica precisely because the content of their gospel challenged the claims of the political powers of the day. They couldn't have been convicted of breaking the law or being insubordinate citizens. They maintained a Christlike submissive posture toward the state. But while being submissive, they were also subversive in their theopolitical claims about Jesus: *We will abide by your laws, not because you are actually in charge but because the Jesus you crucified is in charge and has given you this temporary authority.*

Preaching a spiritual message about a private Jesus who lives in individual hearts doesn't turn the world upside down. Only messages that challenge the ideology of earthly kingdoms do that. We submit to worldly empires for the time being, not because our allegiance is to them but because our allegiance is to the King of creation, who is allowing such rulers to enjoy a brief time of (pseudo)rule.

Paul later wrote two letters to the Thessalonian church, and both are loaded with political language applied to Christ. Paul opens his first letter by celebrating how they had "turned to God from idols" (1:9). This involved all forms of paganism, including the veneration of the emperor, which was popular in Thessalonica.

Paul used other political terms in 1 Thessalonians. For instance, he referred to the "coming" (*parousia*) of Christ the Lord (2:19; 3:13; 4:15; 5:23). The word *parousia* was often used to describe Caesars when they visited a city; we've already looked at how the term "lord" (*kyrios*) was often applied to Caesars as well. The *parousia* of the *kyrios* was common imperial rhetoric. So was the term "meeting," as in 1 Thessalonians 4:17, where Paul described a "meeting" (*apantēsis*) in the air between believers and the Lord. This term was commonly used to describe delegates from a city who would go out to meet an emperor or other dignitary and escort him back to the city.[35] "When Paul *transfers* political language from Caesar to Jesus, who in his view is 'the only God who ever walked the earth,' he makes a political statement, not just a theological one."[36]

When Paul preached the good news that Jesus is King, it rattled people's political perspective. To confess that *Jesus* is King had a profound effect on how someone viewed the authority and power of the earthly empire he or she was living in.

On Passports and Pronouns

We should be cautious about neatly mapping the early church's political situation directly onto our context today. But I think we should be equally cautious about not letting the New Testament's political theology shape our faithfulness today. What could it look like to apply Paul's counter-imperial gospel to our charged political climate today?

One area might be how we view our own citizenship and allegiance to the country where we reside. For instance, I'm a citizen of the United States of America, and I love this country. *Love* is, of course, a strong word with many possible meanings, so let me tease it out. I love this country in the sense that I love many things about the geography and culture of the land where I was born. I love America in the same way that I love baseball, pizza, snowcapped mountains, and sunny beaches. I love the cultural diversity in places like Los Angeles, San Diego, and parts of the San Francisco Bay Area. (Sorry—I'm a Cali boy.) I also love aspects of American history—though, as with all history, America's is a blend of good and evil, racism and democracy, freedom for some and slavery for others. I was born here, and I will probably die here. I'm a citizen of the United States. But this is not my primary identity.

> We live lives of qualified submission to whatever nation God has placed us in, but our allegiance is always to Christ and his global, multi-ethnic kingdom.

As a Christian, my primary identity is that I'm a citizen of Christ's kingdom, which exists throughout the world. I have brothers and sisters, mothers and fathers, scattered across the globe, and my primarily allegiance is to them—to Christ and his global family, which speaks thousands of languages and resides in nearly two hundred countries. Many members of my multi-ethnic family also love many things about the earthly nations they were born in—the geography, culture, food, and sports. But we all live as expatriates among the nations, as strangers and exiles in a foreign land. We live lives of qualified submission to whatever nation God has placed us in, but our allegiance is always to Christ and his global, multi-ethnic kingdom.

We is a seemingly mundane word, but it reveals some interesting assumptions about how Christians view our identity. I'm often struck by how easily Christians in the United States use the pronouns *we, us,* and *our* to refer to our national identity rather than our Christian identity. Many Christians talk about "our country," "our troops," "our borders," and so on. I used to talk like this. But as I kept reading the New Testament, something began to leap off the pages. The first Christians rarely (if ever) used the pronouns *we, us,* and *our* to refer to their relationship with the Roman Empire, even if they were Roman citizens like Paul. It's almost comical to think of Paul referring to the Roman military as "*our* troops" or to the borders of the empire as "*our* borders." Even Roman emperors were never referred to as "our king" or "our leader." They were rulers of a different kingdom, as Paul said in 1 Timothy: "I urge that petitions, prayers, [and] intercessions ... be made for everyone, for kings and all those who are in authority" (2:1–2 CSB). Paul didn't tell Timothy to pray for "our leaders." He told him to pray for Rome's leaders. Christians don't pray for "our leader." We pray *to* our Leader.

How would it reshape our Christian political identity if we reserved plural pronouns for our membership in Christ's global kingdom, rather than using them to describe the earthly nation we happen to have been born into?

Chapter 7

THIS EMPIRE IS NOT OUR HOME

"This world is not our home" is one of the most common tropes in American evangelicalism. It's sometimes followed up with "we're just a-passin' through." This idea comes from certain old hymns and biblical passages like Hebrews 13:14, which, in the New Living Translation, reads, "This world is not our permanent home; we are looking forward to a home yet to come."[1] Some evangelicals take "world" here to mean Planet Earth and believe the "home yet to come" is heaven—a non-earthly place where our souls go when we die and live forever with Jesus.

This interpretation of Hebrews 13:14 conflicts with many other passages in Scripture that talk about the goodness of creation, the resurrection of our bodies, and the renewal of the earth when Jesus returns.[2] When God created the earth, he called it "good" on numerous occasions, and when he created humanity, he fashioned us from the dust of the ground and commissioned us to mediate God's rule over the earth. Humanity was created from the earth and for the earth. In the end, we will live in a new earth with new, physical, resurrected bodies. Contrary to the common trope, this world is quite precisely our home.

Even Hebrews 13:14 agrees. The larger context (and a better translation) of the verse reads:

> Jesus also suffered outside the city gate to make the people holy through his own blood. Let us, then, go to him outside the camp, bearing the disgrace he bore. For here we do not have an enduring city, but we are looking for *the city that is to come.* (vv. 12–14)

"The city that is to come" is elsewhere referred to as "the promised eternal inheritance" (Heb. 9:15), "the city of the living God" (Heb. 12:22), "a kingdom that cannot be shaken" (Heb. 12:28), and "the new Jerusalem," which comes *down from* heaven to God's renewed creation (Rev. 21:1–2). Even Abraham, who lived "like a stranger in a foreign country," was "looking forward to the city"—a physical place—that was to come (Heb. 11:9–10).

Like Abraham and Jesus before us, followers of the Way live in the land but are not of the land. We live as strangers—as exiles—in a foreign country, anticipating a resurrected life in God's already-but-not-yet-fully-here kingdom.

Another passage used to articulate the "earth is not our home" belief comes from 1 Peter, where believers are called "temporary residents" (2:11 NLT). But as in Hebrews, the phrase "temporary residents" doesn't refer to our fleeting life on earth that anticipates our life in heaven, where we really belong. Rather, "temporary residents" is stock Old Testament language for living as exiles in Babylon—a theme that dominates Peter's first epistle.

First Peter is a letter bursting with themes of exile and empire, which begs for an extended inquiry.

Like Abraham and Jesus before us, followers of the Way live in the land but are not of the land.

Christian Exiles Living in Babylon

Peter was writing to a mostly Gentile Christian audience facing some kind of persecution—not full-blown government-sanctioned persecution, but more along the lines of social ostracism and ridicule. Given how much of the letter is devoted to themes surrounding honor and shame, it's likely that the Christian community took seriously Jesus' upside-down kingdom ethic, which turned Rome's hierarchy of social status on its head. Slaves and women were equal to freemen (2:18—3:7),[3] elders were servants rather than celebrities (5:1–5), and all followers of the crucified Christ embraced a virtue utterly despised in Roman eyes: humility (5:5–6; cf. 2:21–25).

"Peter established the readers' value outside of the social system of the dominant culture," writes New Testament scholar Cynthia Long Westfall. "What was disgrace in the eyes of the Roman Empire was honor in the eyes of God and in the community of faith."[4] Christians submitted to governing authorities (2:13–17), but their "nonconformity" was "perceived as a threat to the established order."[5] This is why they were ostracized and ridiculed by people drunk on Roman systems of hierarchy and power.

First Peter is one sustained attempt to rescue Christian exiles from a Babylonian way of life. Peter wasted no time reminding them of their sociopolitical identity. He opens his letter by addressing "God's elect, exiles [*parepidēmos*] scattered [*diaspora*] throughout the provinces of Pontus, Galatia, Cappadocia, Asia and Bithynia" (1:1). This one verse is packed with implications for constructing a Christian political identity and lays the foundation for the theme of exile, which permeates the entire letter.[6]

The word for "exiles" here means just that. While rarely used in Scripture, *parepidēmos* occurs often in literature outside the Bible to refer to someone living in a foreign land.[7] Peter used the term here to highlight the notion that Christians live in a kind of *moral* exile; that is, they live by a different ethical standard and therefore may face ridicule and persecution (e.g., 4:3–4).[8] *Parepidēmos* also includes a sense of political exile, as the next word makes clear.

Diaspora ("dispersed") is clearly drawn from Jewish tradition, where the exiled Jewish people were dispersed among the nations.[9] Stripped of their geopolitical national status, the Jewish exiles had to embody their mission to be a kingdom of priests while living in the shadow of the Babylonian Empire.

Christians should seek the good of the cities
in Galatia or Texas or wherever, but we should
live as if we are exiles living in foreign lands.

Peter believed that his audience was in a similar situation, and he even named the various geographical regions Christians were living in: Pontus, Galatia, Cappadocia, Asia, and Bithynia. This would be like addressing American Christians today as exiles dispersed throughout California, New York, Colorado, and, yes, even Texas. By putting these two terms together—*parepidēmos* ("exile") and *diaspora* ("dispersed")—Peter grabbed the events of the literal Old Testament exile and used them to forge a political identity for his audience. Christians should seek the good of the cities in Galatia or Texas or wherever, but we should live as if we are exiles living in foreign lands.

Peter goes on to command his audience to "live out *the time of your exile* [*ton tēs paroikias humōn chronon*] in reverent fear" (1:17, my translation).[10] And in 2:11, Peter begins a new section in the letter (until 4:11) by reminding Christians that they are "foreigners and exiles" (*paroikous kai parepidēmous*) and are therefore to live differently from the people around them. Both these words overlap in meaning and are probably intended to drive home one concept rather than conveying two different ideas.[11]

The first term, *paroikos*, refers to "a resident alien" or "a foreigner"—someone without full citizenship in the land that they're currently living in.[12] The term occurs thirty-four times in the Old Testament,[13] often referring to Gentiles who lived as foreigners (sometimes translated "sojourners") in the land of Israel. I find it fascinating how many early-church leaders latched on to the term *paroikos* as an apt description of the identity of the church living in the Roman Empire. Clement wrote from "the church of God that *sojourns* at Rome to the church of God that *sojourns* at Corinth." Polycarp wrote to "the church of God that *sojourns* at Philippi." Other Christian writers addressed "the church of God that *sojourns* in Philomelium," "the church that *sojourns* at Gortyna," "the church that *sojourns* at Amastris," and so forth.[14] "'Sojourning' or 'living as aliens' became an identifying mark of the church," writes New Testament scholar J. Ramsey Michaels.[15] Early Christians rightly saw themselves as living in the empire but not being of the empire.

The second term in 1 Peter 2:11 is *parepidēmos*; it describes a person "who has settled in a given place on a temporary basis."[16] Both words together reinforce the believers' identity as not truly belonging to the place where they live. Again, by "place," I don't mean Planet Earth. Believers very much belong here. These two words also don't *just* refer to not belonging to the morally bankrupt society we're surrounded by, though they do include this. The terms can't be divorced from their national and political meanings, rooted in Old Testament narratives about the patriarchs as foreigners among the Canaanites, Israel as oppressed slaves in Egypt, and the southern kingdom of Judah as exiles in Babylon.[17]

Babylon, in fact, is the name Peter gave to the city he was writing from: "She who is in Babylon, chosen together with you, sends you her greetings" (5:13). The "she" here is not a literal woman but the church that Peter belonged to, and "Babylon" was a standard Jewish reference to the city of Rome and its oppressive empire as a whole.[18]

Peter bookends his epistle by mapping the Babylonian exile onto the believers' current status in the empire. This empire is not our home; we're just a-passin' through.

Subversion through Submission

Exiles don't conform to the ways of Babylon, but this doesn't mean we should resist governing authorities, and it certainly doesn't mean we should start a violent revolt. Subversion includes submission, as Peter wrote:

> Submit yourselves for the Lord's sake to every human authority: whether to the emperor, as the supreme authority, or to governors, who are sent by him to punish those who do wrong and to commend those who do right. For it is God's will that by doing good you should silence the ignorant talk of foolish people. Live as free people, but do not use your freedom as a cover-up for evil; live as God's slaves. Show proper respect to everyone, love the family of believers, fear God, honor the emperor. (1 Pet. 2:13–17)

Some scholars point out that submission is different from obedience, but I think this argument can be misleading. The word "submit" here includes obedience to what the human authorities tell us to do (cf. Titus 3:1). Our obedience, however, isn't absolute. There are times when believers are called to disobey governing authorities, as Martin Luther King Jr. famously argued, "One has a moral responsibility to disobey unjust laws."[19] Submission in these cases entails accepting the consequences for civil disobedience.

While we shouldn't separate submission from (qualified) obedience, neither should we equate submission with allegiance. Nowhere in Scripture are exiles called to give their allegiance to Babylon. We submit to Babylon "for the Lord's sake" (1 Pet. 2:13) *because* we give our allegiance to the true King, following in the submissive footsteps of the *true* Emperor (vv. 21–25).

Peter used a quite jarring expression to refer to governing authorities here. The translation above calls them "every human authority," and other translations say "every human institution" (NASB, RSV), but the Greek phrase is *pasē anthrōpinē ktisei*, which literally means "every human *creature*."[20] The word "institution" isn't in the text. Peter did go on to specify that he was talking about emperors and governors (vv. 13–14), so he was talking about governing authorities. But why call them "creatures"? It just so happens that the regions his audience was sojourning in were rife with emperor worship. Perhaps Peter deliberately called the emperor and governor "creatures" as a reminder that they weren't divine. They were created and controlled by the only One who is divine. Christians submit to other creatures whose rule is propped up by the Creator, whose Son sits enthroned "at God's right hand" and looks down on the "authorities and powers in submission to *him*" (3:22).

Exiles and Immigrants

Peter created political distance between the exiled believers and the Roman Empire. When Christians live lives that don't conform to the values of the empire, they should feel like immigrants and foreigners in a strange land. Who better to show the church how to live like this than literal immigrants and foreigners?

Immigration is a hot topic that many Christians divide over, especially in the United States, but I wonder if we're starting these conversations from the wrong place: focusing primarily on what actions we think the nation we're living in should take, instead of focusing on how we're called to live as Christians in exile. As we discussed in chapter 6, it's often revealing (and not in a good way) when Christians use plural pronouns like *we* and *our* to refer to our national identity. Notice how this dynamic plays out as we debate questions like, *How many immigrants should "we" allow to enter "our" country? Which other nations' citizens should "we" prevent from immigrating? Should "we" have stricter border policies or more lenient ones? How should "we" respond to asylum seekers and undocumented immigrants?*

What if we used the plural pronoun *we* to refer to global Christians rather than citizens of Babylon? What if, instead of spending our energy debating whether Babylon should let more Assyrians into Babylon, we made it our mission to embody the

Creator's heart for accepting foreigners and immigrants into our exilic community?

I think we jump the rails when we begin with Babylon's partisan disputes over which policy is more American and then try to plaster some kind of vague Christian-ish rationale on our already-formed opinions. Instead of letting one of Babylon's political parties shape our minds and hearts, what if we started from the perspective of living in exile as immigrants and foreigners ourselves and saw "the other" as more like us than not like us?

For instance, I've grown to know and love a Christian organization called DASH Network, which seeks to embody the love of Christ toward people seeking asylum in the United States. Currently, there's an average two-to-three-year waiting period from the time asylum seekers enter the US to when they receive their permits to work. They're not violating US law during these years; they're going through the legal channels the government has laid out. Yet they're not legally able to work. They're in limbo—not doing anything wrong by the government's standards, yet also not able to work by the same government's standards. The system is broken. Instead of sitting around bickering about it or waiting to vote the right person into office to change the system (which might not be a bad thing), DASH steps in to provide the necessary care for people living in impossible circumstances. Where Babylon's kingdom is failing, Christ's upside-down kingdom is succeeding. At the time of this writing, DASH has provided nearly 3,500 nights of safe housing and more than two million meals for hundreds of people created in God's image.[21]

Instead of letting one of Babylon's political parties shape our minds and hearts, what if we started from the perspective of living in exile as immigrants and foreigners ourselves and saw "the other" as more like us than not like us?

Another beautiful example is that of a small Mennonite church in San Antonio led by pastor John Garland. Several years ago, US Immigration and Customs Enforcement agents bused hundreds of asylum seekers to San Antonio and dropped them off near the Mennonite church. John didn't know what to do, but he had a "core conviction": "It's our building, but it's not really our building. We're going to offer it back to God."[22] John and his members opened up their small church to hundreds of people in need. Political questions surrounding immigration—*Are they here legally? Are they dangerous? Will they hurt America's economy?*—took a back seat to the church's identity as exiles and strangers themselves. The congregation welcomed these asylum seekers into their church and helped provide for their material, spiritual, and psychological needs.

Babylon, by its very nature, will use a border crisis as a political tug-of-war. In the US, the Left accuses the Right of putting vulnerable children in cages. The Right accuses the Left of opening the border to drug dealers and rapists who will hurt the economy and our families. Both sides use fear and anger to foster outrage in your heart and win you to their side. Instead of getting caught up in the culture war, this Mennonite church chose compassion and love. They chose the gospel.

"About 5 to 10 percent of what you hear about in the news is accurate," John told me when I interviewed him on my podcast. He went on: "About 85 percent of the asylum seekers we encountered are evangelical Christians."[23] Though Babylon calls these people foreigners, the gospel calls them family. In other words, *they* are part of *us*—the global body of Christ. And the ones who aren't yet part of our Christian family are still humans in need.

This small Mennonite church engaged politics by first being the political community it hopes to see in the world. It "confront[ed] the world with a political alternative the world would not otherwise know."[24] Rather than being used like pawns in Babylon's culture wars over immigration, this colony of heaven on earth welcomed fellow exiles—members of their global family—to join them in their sojourn in the empire.

When Christians think about immigration and the border crisis, we need to think like exiles, not like Babylonians. We need the same kind of political perspective that ancient Jews might have had if some neighboring Assyrians had crossed the river into the land of Babylon, where the Jews had been exiled—the perspective early

Christians might have had if some Germanic tribes had crossed the border into the land of Galatia, where Peter's exiles were sojourning. Would God's people have been worked up because some fellow foreigners entered the land of their sojourn?

Chapter 8

THE APOCALYPSE OF EMPIRE

The book of Revelation provides us with the most pointed critique of empire in all of Scripture.[1] Revelation was written in the apocalyptic genre—a genre designed to reveal, to peel back the curtain of worldly affairs and show us what's really going on. The apocalyptic genre is "political by nature,"[2] which is why many Jewish writers used it to unmask the real nature of empire.[3] The book of Revelation is therefore "the most powerful piece of political resistance literature from the period of the early Empire."[4] Revelation tells us in the boldest terms what God thinks of empire and how he desires for his followers to live in its shadows.

Not everyone agrees on how to interpret this book, of course. Many Christians today have been trained to interpret Revelation along the lines of Hal Lindsey's *The Late Great Planet Earth* or Tim LaHaye's multi-million-dollar end-times industry sparked by his famous Left Behind books. I won't spend any space reviewing this interpretation, since this isn't how most scholars understand the book. Most importantly, I know of zero experts in first-century Jewish apocalyptic literature who read Revelation this way.

In any case, much of the political relevance I'm going to draw from Revelation won't hang on a particular interpretation of the book as a whole. Some assume that Revelation is all about the future, while others read it as addressing only first-century events. In my survey of literature on Revelation, I'd say that most scholars understand the book as falling somewhere in between these two extremes: it reveals the theological meaning of events most relevant to the first-century church, but it does so in a way that applies to the church of all ages. So the political implications I want to explore won't depend on fringe interpretive views but will be based on readings that are widely agreed on.

The Politics of Revelation

As the previous chapters have shown, the first Christians proclaimed a gospel that clashed with the claims of Rome. This created a rather heated original context for the unabashed critique of empire in the book of Revelation. Its first readers would have had no problem picking up on the subtle—or not-so-subtle—political allusions in the book.

For instance, the frequent mention of "Babylon" clearly refers to Rome. Not only was "Babylon" a common Jewish reference to Rome in the late first century,[5] but John also came right out and said that Babylon, "the mother of prostitutes ... *is* the great city that rules over the kings of the earth" (17:5, 18). None of John's original readers, living at the height of the Roman Empire, would have had any questions about which "great city" John was thinking of.

John also connected Babylon to "a beast ... of the sea," which has ten horns and seven heads (13:1). John later plainly said that "the seven heads *are* seven hills on which the woman sits" (17:9). Rome was widely known as the city on seven hills, and the woman is Babylon/Rome, who is called "the great prostitute" a few verses earlier (v. 1).[6]

Babylon, "the mother of prostitutes" (v. 5), and the beast on which she rides all refer to the Roman Empire or some aspect of it.[7] Revelation scholar Richard Bauckham further teases out John's imagery:

> The beast represents the military and political power of the Roman Emperors. Babylon is the city of Rome, in all her prosperity gained by economic exploitation of the Empire. Thus the critique in chapter 13 is primarily political, the critique in chapters 17–18 primarily economic, but in both cases also deeply religious.[8]

In Revelation 13, John described another beast, one from the land, which serves some kind of religious or priestly function. The land beast "exercised all the authority of the first beast on its behalf, and made the earth and its inhabitants *worship the first beast*" (v. 12).

This second beast most likely refers to "the imperial cults that were so strongly developed in the province of Asia, in which participation was virtually compulsory."[9]

While "nearly all commentators agree that the two Beasts and Babylon symbolize aspects of Roman imperial power,"[10] most go on to point out that these images aren't limited to Rome. "Babylon" refers to Rome, but not *just* Rome: "It also means something more than Rome."[11] Babylon is a flexible concept that can apply to all empires and empire-like nations.

We see this in Revelation 13, where the "beast coming out of the sea" (v. 1) looks like "a leopard" but also has "feet like those of a bear and a mouth like that of a lion" (v. 2). Anyone familiar with the Old Testament knows that these animals (leopard, bear, lion) come straight out of Daniel 7, which describes "four huge beasts" that "came up from the sea, each different from the other" (v. 3 CSB). The first three beasts are described as a lion, a bear, and a leopard (vv. 4–6)—all of which stand for *different empires* (most likely Babylon, Persia, and Greece). Daniel's fourth beast is "terrifying and frightening and very powerful." It has "large iron teeth" and "ten horns" (v. 7). In the context of Daniel, the fourth beast is probably Rome.

But John collapsed all of Daniel's beasts into one beast: a single beast that looks like a leopard, a bear, and a lion. This implies that Babylon *is* Rome, but it's not limited to Rome. Babylon is a concept flexible enough to apply to any number of different empires and nations. Cynthia Long Westfall rightly says that "Rome represents oppressive ungodly power wherever it is located."[12] Michael Gorman likewise says that the two beasts of sea and land "speak of the theopolitical megalomania and of any collaboration of political power and religious sanction—civil religion—that falsely claims to represent the true God and God's will."[13] And Richard Bauckham concludes, "Any society whom Babylon's cap fits must wear it. Any society which absolutizes its own economic prosperity at the expense of others comes under Babylon's condemnation."[14] John's elastic use of "Babylon" in Revelation permits us to refer to America and other empire-like countries today as Babylon.

One of the more daring claims in Revelation is that the Roman government—and other Babylons that wear the same cap—are empowered by Satan. This claim must play a significant role in the church's political theology.

Satan and Empire

In one of the more colorful scenes in Revelation, John sees a dragon that tries to kill Jesus and then goes after his followers (12:1–17). Leaving no room for guessing, John says that "the great dragon" is "that ancient serpent called the devil, or Satan" (v. 9). The spiritual warfare of Revelation 12 takes on political meaning in Revelation 13, when John says that "the dragon [Satan] *gave the beast* [the Roman Empire and others like it] *his power* and his throne and great authority" (v. 2). Again, John writes, "People worshiped the dragon because *he had given authority to the beast*, and they also worshiped the beast and asked, 'Who is like the beast? Who can wage war against it?'" (v. 4).

The Roman Empire was empowered by Satan, and many would worship the empire in light of its seemingly invincible military might: "Who can wage war against it?"

The satanic root of imperial power is a common theme in Scripture. Earlier, we saw that Satan offered Jesus "all the kingdoms of the world and their splendor" (Matt. 4:8), which assumes that Satan had power over those kingdoms. Paul also described earthly rulers being enmeshed with demonic forces when he wrote about powers, thrones, authorities, and rulers.[15] This language refers to "both visible, specific governors *and* the invisible authority exerted by them."[16] Daniel 10 speaks of spirit beings empowering the kingdoms of Persia and Greece (vv. 13, 20). And Isaiah and Ezekiel conflated the rulers of Babylon and Tyre with evil spiritual powers (Isa. 14:12–14; Ezek. 28:12–18).

No first-century Jew or Christian would have been shocked when John attributed Rome's power to Satan.

Modern interpreters living outside of the West also tend to find it easy to accept John's equation of empire with satanic power. It's those of us living in the West, especially in the United States, who struggle most with this reading.[17] We typically have a higher, more positive view of earthly kingdoms than other Christians across the globe. All the more reason for those of us in the West to pay close attention to John's Apocalypse. We especially might need John to peel back the curtain for us to see what's really going on.

Recognizing that the power behind the empire is demonic doesn't mean that every empire or powerful government will be blatantly worshipping Satan, nor does it mean that demonically empowered governments do 100 percent evil 100 percent of the time. Rome did many things that could be considered good. They built an astounding system of roads and kept thieves and robbers at bay, allowing people to travel and commerce to flow. In fact, it was

Rome's system of roads that allowed the gospel to travel far and wide in the first century. Morally, Rome wouldn't tolerate adultery and even made it a punishable crime. Rome valued a certain level of religious freedom; the only religions they wouldn't tolerate were those suspected of sedition. And Rome resonated with some of the same virtues that Christianity upholds—courage, honor, modesty, and self-control—even if they defined some of those virtues differently.

Two things can be true at the same time: governments and empires can accomplish some praiseworthy feats, and they can also be empowered by Satan as Babel-like attempts to rule God's world.

The War of the Lamb

Revelation has a lot to say about politics. It also has a lot to say about war—but not the kind of war some people think of. It's a subversive war where submission is power, weakness is strength, and Christian soldiers in God's upside-down army follow the Lamb wherever he goes. It's a nonviolent war against a violent empire, characterized by submitting to the empire while subverting its ways. Revelation is about subversion through submission as a political act of dissident worship.

The shape of Christ's war against the empire is rooted in Revelation 5, where he appears both as a powerful Lion and as a slaughtered Lamb:

> I wept and wept because no one was found worthy
> to open the scroll or even to look in it. Then one
> of the elders said to me, "Do not weep. Look, the

Lion from the tribe of Judah, the Root of David,
has conquered so that he is able to open the scroll
and its seven seals."

Then I saw one like a slaughtered lamb standing in the midst of the throne and the four living
creatures and among the elders. (vv. 4–6 CSB)

This throne room scene is crucial for understanding the entire
book of Revelation. The interpretive key comes with the contrast
between what John *heard* and what he *saw*. He *heard* about "the
Lion of the tribe of Judah" who has conquered (v. 5), and then he
saw a slain Lamb (v. 6). The contrasting images are significant.

"Lion" and "conquered"—the terms John heard—are militaristic images of warfare, and they conjure up many Old Testament
prophecies about the Davidic Messiah crushing his enemies (e.g., Ps.
2; 110). That's what lions do—they conquer.

But when John turned, he *saw* a slaughtered Lamb (Rev. 5:6),
which is the opposite of a conquering Lion. The contrast between
hearing (a Lion) and *seeing* (a Lamb) is intentional. The images are
mutually interpretive. In the book of Revelation, what John *heard*
is interpreted by what he *saw*. The Lamb, in other words, defines
the manner in which the Lion conquers, as Richard Bauckham
explains:

By juxtaposing the two contrasting images, John
has forged a new symbol of conquest by sacrificial
death. The messianic hopes evoked in 5:5 are not

repudiated: Jesus really is the expected Messiah of David (22:16). But insofar as the latter was associated with military violence and narrow nationalism, it is reinterpreted by the image of the Lamb. The Messiah has certainly won a victory, but he has done so by sacrifice and for the benefit of people from all nations (5:9).[18]

To be clear, the Lamb doesn't express the powerlessness of God. Rather, the Lamb represents divine power reconfigured through submission and sacrifice. Divine power might look like weakness to the world, but when viewed through the lens of God's throne room, the foolishness of the cross embodies the power to conquer. Lamb-ness reveals true Lion-ness.

Christ's sacrificial death, moreover, wasn't just a means to save sinners or pay for our punishment. The Lion/Lamb scene takes place in the divine throne room, the place from which God reigns over his creation. This means that "Christ's sacrificial death *belongs to the way God rules the world*."[19] God's rule clashed with and confronted the way Rome ruled the world. God's Lion-like power was reconfigured through the Lamb's sacrifice, and this is set against the backdrop of Roman power. "Any reading of Revelation—and any practice of theology more generally—that forgets this central New Testament truth is theologically problematic, even dangerous, from its very inception."[20]

Revelation is a book steadily concerned with conquering evil. Yet it says that worldly power isn't the way to do it. Christ conquered evil by submitting to Rome's power, not by imitating it. The divine Lion was unleashed on the dragon by submitting to a Roman cross, and his followers continue to wage war against evil by embodying the same upside-down power of submission and sacrifice (12:11; 15:2).

> ## The question is never, *Should we confront evil?* but rather, *What are the most faithful means by which exiles should confront evil?*

This is one reason why I get nervous when Christians think the best way to conquer evil in the world is by working through Babylon and using Babylonian means of power. How can we trust military power to conquer supposed enemies overseas, or how can we invest in certain government leaders who are clearly using Rome-like power to address whatever evil they believe exists within their empire? Christian exiles who take Revelation seriously should be deeply suspicious of these tactics. The question is never, *Should we confront evil?* but rather, *What are the most faithful means by which exiles should confront evil?*

Divine Power through Sacrifice

The theme of Lion-like divine power manifested in Lamb-like sacrifice is seen throughout Revelation. Chapter 12 says that martyred Christians actually conquer Satan through their sacrificial death:

> They triumphed over [nikaō] him [Satan]
>   by the blood of the Lamb
>   and by the word of their testimony;
> they did not love their lives so much
>   as to shrink from death. (v. 11)

Christians participate in Christ's victory over Satan by bearing witness to the lordship of Christ and by submitting to, not wielding, the sword. This isn't an abstract statement about spiritual warfare; it's a concrete statement about resisting the demonically empowered Roman rule. Revelation 12–13 is all about unveiling the satanic power that's energizing Babylon. Christians who resist the empire incite the dragon, and it may get them killed.

A similar scene occurs in Revelation 15, where Christian martyrs stand with God in heaven because they "had been victorious [nikaō] over the beast and its image and over the number of its name" (v. 2). Roman military language (nikaō) is again turned on its head. True power comes through sacrifice, not military might.

In Revelation 17, the Roman Empire wages "war against the Lamb, but the Lamb will conquer [nikaō] them because he is Lord of lords and King of kings" (v. 14 CSB). Christ has conquered the empire by submitting to their pseudo-power and exposing it as a charade. Like in the throne room scene in Revelation 5, Christ here is revealed as the "Lord of lords and King of kings" who conquers by being conquered. John hijacked the Roman concept of power by turning the term "conquer" on its head.

The Cost of Resisting the Empire

Modern interpreters miss the point if we think early Christians were persecuted because it was illegal for them to believe in their hearts that Jesus is God. It wasn't. Rome was *tolerant* of different religions. Persecution in Revelation wasn't simply religious—at least, not in our modern sense of religion as a private, apolitical endeavor. Persecution was political.[21] If all Christians had done was gather together on Sundays to worship their God, sing songs, and study some religious text, while waving the Roman flag the rest of the week, Rome wouldn't have batted an eye.

Persecution in the early church happened when Christians refused to participate in the imperial cult. This was probably what happened to Antipas, "who was put to death in [Pergamum]—where Satan lives" (Rev. 2:13). The phrase "Satan's throne" (v. 13 CSB) probably describes the massive imperial cult temple that overlooked Pergamum.[22] As John made clear in Revelation 12–13, Satan was behind the imperial cult, and since the Christian message about Christ challenged the authority of the emperors, who sat on "Satan's throne," it's inevitable that the empire would interpret allegiance to Christ as a threat to Rome. Abstaining "from participation in the imperial cults," Greg Carey points out, "would thus mark a person as suspicious. Failure to honor the gods of the empire, including the emperor, detracted from the religious economy that guaranteed their beneficence."[23]

All in all, the Christian way disrupted the values of Rome. Revelation served as a "counter-imperial script," which, as Carey explains, "called Jesus loyalists to an extremely rigorous level of resistance. Their refusal to participate in the imperial cult would isolate them from neighbors, previous associates, perhaps even their previous jobs." And loyalty to Jesus, Carey continues, "would clearly have been tough on anyone involved in buying and selling beyond the merely neighborhood level." Add to all of this the early Christians' "refusal to participate in the imperial cult, which had become part of the regular city political-cultural life."[24] In short, the Christian way of life would have been deemed anti-patriotic on many accounts.

Waving your Bible in one hand and a Roman flag in the other didn't get you persecuted in the first century. But when a religion turned the world upside down by claiming—and living as if—there was another king, one named Jesus, the empire became suspicious.

Babylon's Doom

John's Apocalypse instills hope in the persecuted believers by painting a rather dreadful picture of Babylon's end. Babylon's fate has already been sealed through the crucifixion of the Lamb, who conquers both dragon and beast (4:4–5). We see glimpses of Babylon's final collapse throughout Revelation (14:8; 17:5), but John reserved an entire chapter, Revelation 18, to celebrate God's ruthless judgment on arrogant empires that try to assert their power over creation.

Babylon's sins are many. She's idolatrous, demonic, sexually immoral, violent, and arrogant, and she has hands stained with the blood of Christians. But the most pervasive sins, which take more than half the chapter to describe, are economic in nature. "The merchants of the earth grew rich from her excessive luxuries" (v. 3). She boasts of her great "glory and luxury" (v. 7), and "the kings of the earth ... shared her luxury" (v. 9). When God destroys Babylon,

> the merchants of the earth will weep and mourn over her because no one buys their cargoes anymore—cargoes of gold, silver, precious stones and pearls; fine linen, purple, silk and scarlet cloth; every sort of citron wood, and articles of every kind made of ivory, costly wood, bronze, iron and marble; cargoes of cinnamon and spice, of incense, myrrh and frankincense, of wine and olive oil, of fine flour and wheat; cattle and sheep; horses and carriages; and human beings sold as slaves. (vv. 11–13)

When Babylon's "luxury and splendor have vanished" (v. 14), all the merchants who "gained their wealth from her ... will weep and mourn" the destruction of the great empire that was "dressed in fine linen, purple and scarlet, and glittering with gold, precious stones and pearls" (vv. 15–16).

John's oracle here draws from several passages in Isaiah and Jeremiah that condemn Babylon and from Ezekiel's oracle of judgment against the city of Tyre, which also focuses on economic sins.[25]

It appears that John was doing something similar to what he did in Revelation 13, where he conflated several Old Testament empires into one beast: Babylon. Here too the concept of Babylon is expansive. "If Rome was the heir of Babylon in political and religious activity," writes Richard Bauckham, "she was also the heir of Tyre in economic activity."[26] Thus, "John sees Rome as the culmination of all the evil empires of history" and as "inclusive of all Rome's predecessors."[27] Bauckham sums it up like this:

> Thus the Babylon of Revelation is not only a specific visionary image of contemporary Rome, but also an eschatological image.... It transcends its original reference and becomes a symbol of the whole history of organized human evil whose fall will be the end of history.... So just as Babylon the great includes all Rome's predecessors, so, for us, she must include all Rome's successors in the history of the world's evil empires, political, religious and economic. John's oracle against her is a cap which anyone it fits must wear.[28]

The primary sin that brought Babylon to her death was the idolatry and misuse of wealth. This is why Christians should be slow to celebrate the excessive wealth of the country we're living in. Many of us see a country's wealth as morally neutral, if not a sign of success—perhaps even divine blessing. But according to Revelation, excessive wealth led to Babylon's arrogance, sexual immorality, and indulgence. Particular attention is given to the many luxury items that flowed into Babylon from other parts of the world: gold, silver, pearls, precious stones, purple, silk, ivory, costly wood, marble, and exotic spices. Where did these come from? What happened to the places where these luxury items were derived? Did any injustices occur along the way to funnel these unnecessary luxuries into the homes of the wealthy?

> Citizens of Christ's global kingdom should have global concerns, not just nationalistic interests.

Christians should ask the same questions of the Babylons we're living in. An empire's economic system isn't neutral, and moral questions go far beyond "What policies will make Babylon and its citizens the wealthiest?" Citizens of Christ's global kingdom should have global concerns, not just nationalistic interests. And we should be nervous when the nation we're living in becomes excessively wealthy.

Cultivating an Apocalyptic Political Posture

The book of Revelation is essential for shaping our Christian political identity. The overarching exhortation is one of resistance and submission. We resist Babylon's idolatry. We denounce its sexual immorality. We separate ourselves from its intoxicated quest for luxury and splendor. We don't become enamored with Babylon's military strength. We proclaim a different King and celebrate a different way of life. Citizens of God's kingdom follow the way of the Lamb by loving our enemies, serving those around us, caring for the poor, and testifying to the wisdom of God by embodying his multi-ethnic reign on earth.

Christians also have a very different view of power from the world around us. We see this in Deuteronomy 17's portrayal of the ideal king. We see it in Jesus' pervasive teachings about the first being last and servants being leaders. We see it as crucifixion becomes a means of defeating dragons. Christians have a very different way of confronting evil and ruling the world.

This is one of the many reasons for concern when the kingdom of God becomes entangled with the kingdoms of this world. As Nilay Saiya writes, "When the church becomes entangled with political power ... it loses its prophetic potential."[29] Citizens of God's kingdom bear witness to the power of God through sacrifice and submission. Meanwhile, the kingdoms of this earth rule the world by relying on worldly power—the very power Christ renounced through his life, his teaching, and especially his death. Whatever involvement Christians have with the kingdoms of this world, we must live as people who belong to a different kingdom empowered by sacrifice, forgiveness, reconciliation, and enemy love. We can't seek to defeat the dragon using dragon-like power, nor should we put our trust in earthly rulers who look more like the beast than the Lamb. We look forward not to the day when Babylon will be great, but to the day when God will destroy all empires on earth to make way for his eternal kingdom—a kingdom that is already breaking into history through the global countercultural church.

Whatever involvement Christians have with the kingdoms of this world, we must live as people who belong to a different kingdom empowered by sacrifice, forgiveness, reconciliation, and enemy love.

Chapter 9

EXILE AS PROPHETIC WITNESS

Our journey thus far has shown that God's people were called to view themselves as politically distinct from the nations around them. Even when Israel was an actual nation, they were to be different from the other nations. Their exile to Babylon galvanized their distinct political identity, with the people of God continuing to live *in* the nations but not *of* them. This theme runs right on through the rest of the Bible, as "the entire New Testament is written from the perspective of exile."[1] Sometimes the language of exile is explicit (in 1 Peter and Revelation, for example), and at other times the concept is present while the exact wording is not.

What I want to do now is pull some of these pieces together by looking at the relationship between church and state through a wide-angle lens. Specifically, I want to consider how the theme of exile informs the global church's political identity in relation to the state. Christians throughout history have debated the church's relationship to the state, and many views have been put forward.[2] My goal here is not to be thorough or dogmatic but to be more suggestive and heuristic. Basically, I want to gather what I've learned from the biblical narrative and ask the question: Inasmuch as I've read Scripture correctly, how should the modern church live as exiles in the shadow of the empire?

I'll wrestle with this question by describing three overarching views of the relationship between church and state: Detachment, Transformation, and Prophetic Witness.[3] The first two, Detachment and Transformation, can be seen as the opposite ends of a spectrum of political engagement. There will, of course, be wide variations among people who hold each view, which is why thinking in terms of a spectrum is more helpful than separating the two into airtight, monolithic categories. The third view, Prophetic Witness, tries to capture the best of both Detachment and Transformation while weeding out some of the problems inherent in them.

Three Approaches to Church and State

Detachment

The Detachment view emphasizes the church's separateness from society. On the spectrum of political engagement, Detachment represents the low end of the spectrum: as little political engagement as possible. In the US, a strong form of this approach is seen in Amish communities, which seek to exist wholly separate from the secular cities around them. While relatively few Christians in the West are as dedicated to Detachment as the Amish, there are also many more popular versions of Detachment that emphasize the church's separateness from society.

Many (though not all) Christians who adopt the Detachment lens see the church's mission as wholly spiritual rather than material. In other words, they believe Christians should focus on saving souls and not concern themselves with social justice or trying to make the world a better place. Doing so, they might argue, would be like rearranging deck chairs on a sinking ship. This world is not our home, and it's all going to burn anyway. Our home is in heaven, so the goal of our fleeting earthly existence is to get as many souls up to heaven as we can.

Keeping oneself unstained from the world also tends to be a top priority in the Detachment view. More conservative forms of this view might take a homeschool-only approach to education, create Christian-only sports clubs, listen only to Christian music, and watch only Christian movies. Other less conservative forms of Detachment emphasize the social and political bankruptcy of the world around us and the need for the church to remain separate from these evil systems, without embracing a "heaven is our home; it's all going to burn anyway" kind of theology.

There are many things to commend in the Detachment view. For instance, I appreciate the concern for purity and holiness, and I applaud the emphasis on living lives that look different from the world around us. And I think certain forms of Detachment that highlight the evil of political systems resonate with the scriptural perspective.

I do, however, have some reservations about this view, or at least about certain ways it can misapply the Bible's invitation to exilic living.

First, the purity of the church isn't an end in itself; rather, the church should be holy because it's a kingdom of priests and a light to the nations. Holiness has a missional purpose—to bear witness to the reign of God *in order to show* the world what it means to live as a multi-ethnic global community. Insofar as holiness is viewed as an end in itself, the Detachment view falls short of the mission of the church.

Second, I think some forms of Detachment can border on Gnosticism when they focus on reaching human *souls* but don't meet material needs. The parable of the good Samaritan is a classic reminder of the truth that meeting physical needs is an inherent good in itself. Humans are more than just souls; we are embodied souls and ensouled bodies. The material creation is *good* (Gen. 1), and so are our bodies, as the doctrines of incarnation and resurrection show. God is on a mission not simply to save human souls but to redeem his material creation (Rom. 8:19–23) and usher in a new creation (Rev. 21–22).

Third, I find that some forms of Detachment have a skewed theology of empire. Put simply, they don't view empire as bad, just left-wing versions of it. They might even use the language of exile to describe their identity, but in their view, they've been exiled from the conservative culture that we used to live in, where family values were cherished, abortion was illegal, and conservatives were in charge of the country. What's needed is for the church to keep ourselves unstained by the evil of society while *teaming up with right-wing parties to end our exile.*

I don't think this captures the biblical view of empire, however. As we've seen throughout Scripture, empire as a whole is problematic, not just certain forms of empire. We don't see the church resisting empire by collaborating with who they think are the best rulers of the empire; rather, we see God's people embodying God's kingdom as a form of submissive resistance toward the empires they were living under. In short, I wish conservative Christians would be more suspicious of right-wing quests to gain power in Babylon. (I'm equally concerned with progressive Christians not being more suspicious of left-wing quests to gain power in Babylon.)

> We don't see the church resisting empire by collaborating with who they think are the best rulers of the empire.

Lastly, inasmuch as the Detachment view focuses on holiness and not on addressing injustices, I think it falls short of the church's vocation in the world. Throughout Scripture, the prophets called out their own nation *and the nations around them* when they abused their power. The kinds of evil they called out often had to do with what we might now consider social justice: judicial systems that favored the rich, the mistreatment of the poor and marginalized, and the abuse of power by those in leadership.[4] The book of Revelation calls on God's people to come out of Babylon while also calling Babylon out for her many injustices (Rev. 18). Living as exiles doesn't mean we don't care about injustice in Babylon. It means we cultivate the most Christlike means of caring.

It's this last point that leads to the other end of the spectrum: the Transformation view. Once they've recognized the Christian necessity of caring about injustice, some people feel that they are morally obligated to respond to that injustice through the best means available to them, and these appear to be political means. Hence the need for the church to transform political systems in order to address injustice in the world.

TRANSFORMATION

The Transformation view believes that "Christians have a responsibility to bring 'Christian values' to bear in all areas of life and to engage the world in all its dimensions, including the economic, social, and political arenas."[5] In their mission to transform all areas of life, Christians have a duty to engage political systems. After all, they argue, God created governments to establish justice, reward good behavior, and punish bad behavior. God has given governments the right to "bear the sword" (Rom. 13:4; cf. 1 Pet. 2:13–17) and execute vengeance on those who do evil (Gen. 9:6). "Christians, therefore, can participate in the transformation of the earthly city through their political activities and, in this way, help advance the kingdom of God by continuing the task given to Adam and Eve in the Garden of Eden before the Fall."[6]

To be clear, the Transformation view is bipartisan; there are both right-wing and left-wing forms of it. Right-wing versions seek to transform society through empowering right-wing political leaders and policies, while left-wing forms do the same through empowering left-wing political leaders and policies. Obviously, the things they're advocating for look quite different, but the means are similar. Change comes through the channels of Babylon's political system. While we can't legislate the kingdom of God into existence, Christians should be politically involved as an expression of neighborly love. To not care about secular politics is to not care about people, since the decisions the government makes have massive effects on the lives of the people we're called to love.

Typically, right-wing versions of this approach say that Christians should give their allegiance to God while also pledging their allegiance to the state, since we are called to be loyal to both God and country. Left-wing versions don't sound as patriotic, but they still tend to believe that evil exists primarily on the Right and that the most practical ways of defeating such evil is by supporting the Left. In a subtler way, this approach still gives its allegiance to the state; it invests the state with the power to conquer evil, establish justice, and care for the poor.

I appreciate many things about the Transformation view. It rightly views holiness not just in terms of personal morality but also in terms of social justice. I'm sympathetic to the concern that certain policies of Babylon affect real people—especially the poor and disenfranchised. History is filled with examples of the church confronting societal evils by working to change certain systems within the empire. Christians helped end chattel slavery in both the

UK and the US, and they played a significant role in the civil rights movement in the twentieth century. On the flip side, many German Christians were either silent about or complicit in the Nazi rise to power that led to the Third Reich. There certainly do seem to be times when the church should address societal evils, which might include seeking to change unjust laws and evil systems.

To my mind, Martin Luther King Jr. represents the Transformation view at its best. For instance, he pointed out in a speech addressing the Voting Rights Act,

> It may be true that the law can't make a man love
> me, but it can restrain him from lynching me.
> And I think that's pretty important also. So while
> the law may not change the hearts of men, it does
> change the habits of men.[7]

MLK rightly carved out a place for healthy and righteous civic involvement. The church can and should pursue justice in the world and seek the good of the city.

But MLK and the civil rights movement as a whole, while not perfect, sought to instill Christian values through Christian means. The civil rights movement imitated not the power of the beast but the power of the Lamb as it sought to achieve justice through nonviolent enemy love. It submitted to the state, even while calling the state to justice. It didn't give allegiance to Babylon or to one of Babylon's political parties. The movement was, from what I can tell, nonpartisan. It didn't demand that participants join a political party or view another political party as evil. At its core, it addressed Babylon's injustices by using Christlike means of subversive submissiveness. Some might even consider MLK and the civil rights movement to be closer to the Prophetic Witness perspective articulated below.

When we call Babylon to justice, it's from the perspective of belonging to a different kingdom and serving a different King, who's ruling the world through the radically different means of sacrifice, love, and forgiveness.[8]

While there are many things to commend in the Transformation view, certain forms of it could face some challenges.

First, I'm not sure that it takes seriously enough a biblical theology of empire; specifically, Scripture's pervasive theme that governments have been co-opted by Satan (e.g., Dan. 10; Matt. 4; Rev. 12–13). Yes, our sovereign God can certainly use these governments to carry out his will, and again, we're called to submit to governing authorities (Rom. 13:1–7). But theologically, citizens of God's kingdom should at least be cautious of, and sometimes even opposed to, working in and through the demonically empowered authorities of earth to bring justice to the world. Through the lens of Revelation, this would be like working with a dragon-empowered beast to defeat … the dragon?

Second, Scripture says that God redeems people, not worldly systems and kingdoms that compete with his reign. In other words, God will redeem Babylonians, but he will judge Babylon as a system of rule. I think Nilay Saiya is correct when he points out that "New Testament authors speak of people, not political orders, as being the recipients of God's grace and the church as the only present institution that God redeems."[9] The kingdom of God is never described as partnering with the kingdom of Babylon. According to Daniel,

God's kingdom "will crush all those kingdoms and bring them to an end, but it will itself endure forever" (2:44). Revelation celebrates God's destruction of Babylon (Rev. 18), as did many prophets of old. It's one thing to be civically involved and call out injustice when we see it, but we should keep in mind that the empire we're seeking to reform will always be Babylon and not the new Jerusalem.

Third, I'm perhaps most concerned about the political allegiances often formed in the Transformation view. When our allegiance is to a particular political party or candidate, this inevitably fosters a kind of antagonism toward their opponent and all who voted for them. Such an "us versus them" perspective hinders the church's unity and witness in the world. When Christ-followers disagree over which Babylonian leader will do a better job leading Babylon, this shouldn't interfere with their unified mission to make known "the manifold wisdom of God ... to the rulers and authorities" (Eph. 3:10)—but it often does. Political divisions in the church have wreaked havoc on the church's mission.

Such partisan allegiances also foster a kind of misplaced hope. We see this every four years during the US presidential elections, where one candidate is viewed as the Devil and the other achieves near-messianic status as the one who will defeat evil. The 2020 election was particularly telling, on both sides of the political aisle. Some of my Republican friends were so horrified at the evils on the Left that they invested tremendous hope in the admittedly morally bankrupt Donald Trump to defeat the Left. Some of my left-wing friends did the same: they were so horrified at Trump—and all those who voted for him—that they put their hope in Joe Biden to defeat him. If Trump is the Antichrist, then Biden becomes a kind of Christ figure. Or if Biden is the Devil, then Trump must be some kind of messiah. To defeat the Left/Right, we must empower the Right/Left.

Such partisan allegiances also foster a kind of misplaced hope.

I think both perspectives dilute the church's hope in King Jesus. Throughout the New Testament, the proclamation that Jesus is Lord meant that Caesar was not. In a similar way, our hope in Jesus as the true King casts a shadow over any kind of hope we might put in the powers and authorities of this present age. This doesn't mean some Babylonian leaders aren't better at managing Babylon than others; we just need to keep reminding ourselves that they're managing *Babylon*. And it certainly doesn't mean we shouldn't care about the injustices around us. It just means our civic involvement should be an extension of our allegiance to Christ and his kingdom, not a distraction from it—a tension we'll tease out below when we discuss the Prophetic Witness view.

One objection I often hear when I raise concerns over the Transformation view is that Christians didn't have the same opportunity to get involved in the government in the first century as many of us do today. Rome wasn't a democracy. Christians couldn't vote or run for office. As a tiny religious movement, Christianity didn't have any power to effect change in Rome. But Christians (in the US, at least) are in a very different situation. We can vote. We can be involved. We can run for office or vote in people who will effect change. Therefore, we can't take the early church's relationship to Rome and map it onto the US church's situation today.

It's true that there are many differences between the Roman Empire and the United States and between the first-century church and the twenty-first-century church. (There are many similarities as well!)[10] But I think this pushback overreaches in its critique.

First, it assumes that if the first-century church did have the opportunity to effect change through Babylonian channels, it would have. The closest thing in the New Testament to modern political parties are the Jewish sects of Pharisees, Sadducees, Herodians, and Zealots. Whenever they tried to find out which "side" Jesus was on, he didn't play their game. He wasn't on any of their sides. He was establishing an alternative kingdom that was wholly different from whatever mini-kingdom these Jewish sects were trying to establish. Jesus showed a confident indifference to the political affairs of his day, not because he didn't care about justice but precisely because he did. Jesus believed that true justice and righteousness would be established through a different, upside-down kingdom.

Second, even though the context is different, the Bible still provides us with enough political theology to shape the church's posture toward all forms of government. We must take the principles about living in the shadow of the empire and apply them to our current situation. We don't need a one-to-one correspondence between, say, Rome and the United States to draw relevance from the Bible's theology of empire. The church's exilic posture toward Babylon was held not simply for pragmatic reasons but also for theological ones. And as we saw in the book of Revelation, the concept of Babylon, while referring immediately to Rome, is designed to apply to all Babylon-like empires.[11]

In short, we don't need modern empire-like nations to look exactly like Rome in order for them to be Babylon in the biblical sense.

> Jesus believed that true justice and righteousness would be established through a different, upside-down kingdom.

Third, throughout history, the Christian church did have opportunities to partner with the empire, and we often took those opportunities. Looking back, we must ask, How did that go for us? When the emperor Constantine allegedly became a Christian, the church jumped from being a persecuted people to occupying positions of power. By most Christian standards of measurement, this didn't go well for the church.[12] It "had the effect of compromising the church's distinctiveness and landing a severe blow to its gospel witness, transforming Christianity into a political ideology and its institutions into political interest groups."[13] The radical ethic of peace, sacrifice, and enemy love is incompatible with the coercive power of earthly governments. When followers of the Lamb join the beast in an effort to transform society, they often end up looking more like a beast than a Lamb.

History has shown us many examples of the church gaining power from the state, and as far as I can tell, it has never ended well for the church. Examples can be found in the history of Russia, China, Argentina, Rwanda, Uganda, Zambia, and other countries where the church gained political power. In Guatemala, for instance, the Christian dictator Efraín Ríos Montt "used the Bible to justify the mass murder of political opponents" (more than eighty-six thousand of them).[14] It's almost always the case that when the church becomes too enmeshed with the power of the state, the upside-down kingdom of God is turned right side up.[15] Christianity is simply not designed to occupy positions of worldly power without betraying its mission and witness.

Whatever civic involvement the church pursues, we must do so *as the church*, as outposts of heaven on earth, as citizens of an upside-down kingdom—as exiles in Babylon.

PROPHETIC WITNESS

The third approach is what Nilay Saiya calls Prophetic Witness, which believes that "Christ has called his followers to form an alternative political community that lives in contradiction to the world, yet not aloof from it—to be in the world but not of it."[16]

Like the Detachment view, Prophetic Witness prioritizes the church's distinctiveness from the world. The upside-down kingdom of God looks very different from the kingdoms of this world. The key difference is that the Prophetic Witness view advocates for cultural engagement and social justice—values it shares with the Transformation view. But unlike the Transformation view, Prophetic Witness is far more reluctant to get entangled with Babylon's systems of power to bring about change in the world.

Within the Prophetic Witness framework, the church cares deeply about justice but is suspicious about teaming up with Babylon to achieve it. If the church has the opportunity to reform the state, work with the state to pursue good, or establish justice in society, it must do so *as the church*—as imitators of the crucified Lamb, whose power is derived from sacrifice and self-giving love. The exiled church doesn't battle the beast by using beast-like means of coercion and worldly power. "Prophetic Christianity," writes Saiya, "fundamentally distrusts and resists the state and maintains its distance from it; it challenges the powers instead of trying to replace them."[17] This doesn't mean the church never interacts with the state. It means our interaction "takes the form of ad hoc, discriminating engagement in which the church makes no effort to cultivate a relationship of privilege with the powers."[18]

Stanley Hauerwas and William Willimon articulate this perspective when they say that "the political task of Christians is to be the church," to engage the world "with a political alternative the world would not otherwise know."[19] The question is not *whether* we engage the world around us but *how* we engage. Being the church is the best, most faithful means by which we influence the world. The church is "an alternative *polis*," or city, that "seeks to influence the world by being the church, that is, by being something the world is not and can never be, lacking the gift of faith and vision, which is ours in Christ."[20] If the church fails to embody the way of the cross—sacrifice, forgiveness, enemy love—in our pursuit of justice, then we declare to the world that Jesus and his kingdom are irrelevant for establishing justice in the world.[21]

The Prophetic Witness view is especially critical of partisan politics and giving allegiance to either side of Babylon's political aisle. This can sometimes be interpreted as centrist or politically moderate; it is neither left nor right, neither Republican nor Democrat. The critique often follows that such a view lacks conviction. By failing to pick a side, a centrist position does little to stand against injustice and lets evil run rampant.

This critique can come from both sides of the partisan aisle. Conservatives might say that anyone who is insufficiently conservative fails to take a stand against abortion, sexual immorality, and sex change operations for minors. Meanwhile, progressives might accuse anyone who is insufficiently progressive of being indifferent toward racism, misogyny, homophobia, xenophobia, and the lack of basic health care for all. Both sides can look at anyone who appears centrist and say, "Your silence is complicity."

No matter what direction this critique comes from, it is based on the same belief: The best way to defeat the evil from the Left is by joining arms with the Right. Or the best way to defeat the evil from the Right is by joining arms with the Left.

But I think the assumptions driving this critique are still stuck in a Babylonian way of interpreting the world. The Prophetic Witness view isn't moderate or centrist, because *it doesn't situate its political identity somewhere on the spectrum of Babylon's political options.* Prophetic witnesses are on a different spectrum altogether. They're not left or right, but this doesn't make them centrist or moderate. They're up, or down, or diagonal.

The Prophetic Witness view resists the spectrum of options created by Babylon—left, right, center. It believes that the church can be concerned about evils that exist on one side of the political spectrum without thinking that the other side is particularly faithful in confronting those evils. Christians are invited to see the world through a different lens. We view it through the cross, where sacrifice is power, humility is honor, and loving your enemies conquers dragons.

We can have opinions on Babylon's cultural issues: abortion, war, immigration, sexuality, health care, and so on. But we are called to view these issues through the lens of the cross rather than through Babylon's tribalistic lenses. Communities of the cross should absolutely care about justice and confront oppression. It's part of our identity. Yet we don't just follow Babylon's script of what this caring must look like. We pursue justice and righteousness *by being* the community of the Lamb—by embodying the kind of *polis* most citizens are trying to vote into existence.

To give one concrete example of what this can look like, let's take the debate over guns. One of the most hotly debated political topics in the US right now has to do with gun rights and gun violence. Since 1970, there have been more than 20,000 gun deaths per year—and the number keeps increasing. In 2021, 48,830 people were killed by a gun.[22] Naturally, this reality has turned into a huge political debate. The Left wants stricter gun laws and bans on assault weapons to reduce gun violence. The Right says that most people use handguns to kill people, not assault weapons, and the criminals often come from broken families; they argue that what's needed is for fathers to stop leaving their families and for stricter penalties for gun violence. Plus, the Right observes, states like Illinois already have strict gun laws, yet Chicago is still plagued by gun violence. The Left responds by pointing out that Chicago borders Indiana, which has looser gun laws, so people can just drive a few minutes to the next state to buy guns; what's needed are stricter gun laws on a federal level.

So the debate rages on, and Christians line up like sheep behind their favorite political party to *baa* their tribe's talking points.

Meanwhile, a group of Christians in Chicago have gathered together to address the violence in their neighborhoods through a different means—*being the church* by pursuing justice in the world. Together Chicago is an organization founded by Michael Allen and David Dillon, two Christians who have a passion for addressing gun violence in their city. They saw that gun violence was complex and that arguing over policies and politics wouldn't be enough to actually bring about change in Chicago. So they pulled together various nonprofit, government, business, faith, and community leaders to form a collective addressing the complex issues that fuel gun violence. Their organization targets five areas of social engagement: economic development, education, violence reduction, gospel justice, and faith-community mobilization. Each of these issues is related to gun violence in Chicago. As Together Chicago mobilizes various leaders to address the issue of violence, they express their commitment to the lordship of Jesus.

Participants describe their mission this way: "With God's help, his people together are transforming Chicago."[23]

West Haven Park is a neighborhood in Chicago that has felt the impact of both gun violence and Together Chicago's work. By addressing the various factors that lead to gun violence, the Christians of Together Chicago have made the world around them a better place. "Through multiple community and church partnerships, the neighborhood is now safer. Mothers and children are outside enjoying local parks for the first time in years." Together Chicago has, in the words of one participant, "[brought] the church to the streets."[24]

Together Chicago is a great example of God's people engaging the political world in a way that effects real change. And they are doing it without depending on Babylon's levers of power. Maybe voting the right candidate into office will help alleviate gun violence in Chicago. Or maybe it won't. Babylonian politicians might continue to use the violence in Chicago as a pawn in their political games. Meanwhile, Together Chicago isn't putting their hope in the best Babylonian leader to institute the best policy to reduce gun violence—whatever that policy may be. Rather, they are *being the church* in a small slice of creation that's ruled by King Jesus.

Far from being apolitical, the church is called to be the political community it wishes to see in the world.

What about Romans 13?

One of the most common pushbacks I hear is "What about Romans 13?"[25] The question assumes that Romans 13 and other similar texts encourage Christians to view the state in a more positive light. The relevant portion reads,

> Let every person be subject to the governing authorities. For there is no authority except from God, and those that exist have been instituted by God. Therefore whoever resists the authorities resists what God has appointed, and those who resist will incur judgment. For rulers are not a terror to good conduct, but to bad. Would you have no fear of the one who is in authority? Then do what is good, and you will receive his approval, for he is God's servant for your good. But if you do wrong, be afraid, for he does not bear the sword in vain. For he is the servant of God, an avenger who carries out God's wrath on the wrongdoer. Therefore one must be in subjection, not only to avoid God's wrath but also for the sake of conscience. (vv. 1–5 ESV)

Some Christians cite Romans 13 in defense of things like the death penalty, voting, military funding, and government involvement in general. But I think this approach misinterprets what Paul was actually saying. Far from advocating for Christian support of the state, Romans 13 encourages Christians to submit to an oppressive empire that God is using to carry out his will *and* that God will destroy in the end (Rev. 17–19).

It's important to note that Romans 13 comes after Romans 12 (there were no chapter divisions in Paul's original letter). And in Romans 12, Paul gave a litany of commands that shape the church's posture in the world: "Do not conform to the pattern of this world" (v. 2). "Hate what is evil; cling to what is good" (v. 9). "Bless those who persecute you; bless and do not curse" (v. 14). "Do not be proud" (v. 16). "Associate with people of low position" (v. 16). "Do not be conceited" (v. 16). "As far as it depends on you, live at peace with everyone" (v. 18). "If your enemy is hungry, feed him; if he is thirsty, give him something to drink" (v. 20). "Do not be overcome by evil, but overcome evil with good" (v. 21). This is the stuff of an upside-down kingdom—like a mini version of Christ's Sermon on the Mount. When we get to Romans 13, we must bring Romans 12 with us. *This* is the posture of citizens of Christ's kingdom, and it looks very different from the posture of citizens of this world.

Unlike Romans 12, which gives more than twenty-five commands to the church, Romans 13:1–5 gives one: "Let everyone be subject to the governing authorities" (v. 1).[26] Romans 12 seeks to cultivate in the church a humble, peaceful, Christlike posture, which empowers the church to defeat the empire by submitting to it. Whatever involvement Christians have with the empire, it must come with a Romans 12 posture.

One of the starkest contrasts between the two chapters becomes clear when we compare Romans 12:19 to 13:4. Together, they read,

> Beloved, never **avenge** yourselves, but leave it to
> the **wrath of God**, for it is written, "Vengeance
> is mine, I will repay, says the Lord." (12:19 ESV)

For he [Rome] is the servant of God, an avenger
who carries out God's wrath on the wrongdoer.
(13:4b ESV)

Romans 12:19 commands the church to never take vengeance,
leaving it to God's wrath. Romans 13:4 tells us *how* God takes
vengeance and carries out his wrath. In other words, Romans 12
prohibits Christians from doing the very thing God does in Romans
13—executing vengeance and wrath.

There's nothing in Romans 13 that encourages Christians to
be involved with the government or use the levers of governmental
power to accomplish Christian good in the world. Perhaps there are
other passages that do this, but Romans 13 isn't one of them.

Paul did call Rome "God's servant" in Romans 13:4, and this
may sound as if Paul was optimistic about the government, speaking
positively of Rome's rule. Such pro-government readings of Romans
13 should be tempered by other passages that refer to Rome as a
satanically empowered beast ruled by harlots who are drunk on power,
violence, and luxury and who are destined to destruction (e.g., Rev.
13; 17–18). In any case, the phrase "God's servant" isn't as positive as it
may sound. It actually comes from the Old Testament prophets, who
often talked about God working through some rather evil nations to
carry out his will. The Old Testament refers to several political figures
as God's servant, such as Nebuchadnezzar, king of Babylon (Jer. 27:6;
43:10); Cyrus, king of Persia (Isa. 44–45); and the ruthlessly wicked
nation of Assyria, which God called "the club of my wrath" and "the
rod of my anger" (Isa. 10:5). Cyrus, Nebuchadnezzar, and others were

ruthless pagan dictators. God wasn't praising them. Rather, he was asserting his sovereignty over them.

Romans 13 is situated in this prophetic tradition. *Therefore, the phrase "God's servant" refers not to Rome's sanctified service to God but to God's sovereign ability to use an evil empire as an instrument in his hands.* Romans 13 isn't as much pro-government as it is pro-God, and followers of God should take seriously the stark differences between his kingdom and the kingdom of Babylon.

First Peter 2:13–17, which we looked at in chapter 7, is another passage sometimes taken to support a more positive view of the state:

> Submit yourselves for the Lord's sake to every human authority: whether to the emperor, as the supreme authority, or to governors, who are sent by him to punish those who do wrong and to commend those who do right. For it is God's will that by doing good you should silence the ignorant talk of foolish people. Live as free people, but do not use your freedom as a cover-up for evil; live as God's slaves. Show proper respect to everyone, love the family of believers, fear God, honor the emperor.

As with Romans 13, Peter said nothing more than that the church should submit to governing authorities and honor (not slander) earthly rulers, since we are to "show proper respect to everyone" (1 Pet. 2:17). There's no command or encouragement for Christians to work through Babylonian channels to bring about kingdom values on earth. Again, I'm not saying Peter was forbidding this work. He just wasn't arguing in favor of it.

Plus, this passage is situated in the middle of a letter where Peter called the church "exiles" (1:1), "foreigners" (1:17), and "foreigners and exiles" (2:11). He explicitly called Rome "Babylon" (5:13). The church's submissive posture toward Babylon is shaped by their identity as exiles and foreigners. Like the literal Jewish exiles in Jeremiah's day, Christians are to be good citizens, seek the good of the city they live in, and submit to governing authorities, because they are exiles who belong to a different kingdom.

I don't believe Romans 13 or 1 Peter 2 encourages Christians to collaborate with Babylon to bring about kingdom values in the world. Instead, both passages assume a marked dissonance between the kingdom of God and the governments of the world.

What about Joseph, Daniel, and Esther?

But what about instances where we find faithful believers like Joseph, Daniel, and Esther working for the state?[27] Not only did God use them to help the nations they were involved with, but they also seemed to be on quite friendly terms with at least some governing rulers.

There are at least two reasons I don't think these examples are as pro-political-involvement as they initially appear. First, all three figures were taken against their will. Joseph was bought as a slave by Potiphar, one of Pharaoh's officials. It's not as if he pursued government work or ran for office. Daniel too was taken by the oppressive empire of Babylon after they slaughtered thousands of men, women, and children, while exiling many more to serve the interests of a pagan state. Esther was a victim of royal power, as she was taken into the king's harem to serve his sexual appetite and display his wealth. None of these instances seem to be good examples of patriotism toward the state. If anything, the dark shadow of oppressive empires looms large in these stories.

Second, both Joseph and Daniel maintained strict fidelity to God, which sometimes led to deliberate opposition from the state. Joseph stood by his Jewish values (i.e., he rejected the sexual advances of Potiphar's wife), which landed him in prison, and Daniel kept his Jewish dietary restrictions and disobeyed various laws that nearly cost him his life on several occasions. The ethics of Esther are notoriously complicated, as scholars debate whether her actions are meant to be praised or criticized.[28] In any case, the main point of the book appears to be not pro-Persia but pro-Yahweh—who, although unnamed in the book, was still caring for his people while they lived in an oppressive foreign nation.

In short, I don't think Joseph, Daniel, and Esther are great examples of patriotism toward the state. Instead, they are examples of the scriptural principle that believers "must obey God rather than human beings" (Acts 5:29). If we are taken into positions of governmental power against our will, we must maintain fidelity to God even if the state throws us to the lions.

Conclusion

I do believe the Prophetic Witness perspective captures the best parts of the Detachment and Transformation views regarding the church and state. It prioritizes the church's holiness and distinctiveness from the surrounding culture, as the Detachment view rightly emphasizes. Yet it also values the Transformation view's concern to seek the good of the city and address injustices in the world, without getting too entangled in Babylon's political power games. Most of all, at least to my mind, the Prophetic Witness perspective seems to resonate most with how believers throughout Scripture were called to position themselves in the shadow of empire.

Chapter 10

LIVING AS EXILES IN BABYLON

In this final chapter, I want to wrestle with what it might look like for Christians to live as exiles in the shadow of empire. The word *might* here is important. I don't intend to preach a dogmatic, black-and-white, "here's how everyone must live" sort of sermon. Rather, I'd like to offer some of my own raw reflections as I sit back and ask myself, *In light of everything we've seen in Scripture thus far, how should we think about things like voting, political parties, the Pledge of Allegiance, and other boots-on-the-ground politically related questions?* My goal isn't to be exhaustive; I'm not going to argue for the best health care policy or talk about how to end climate change. As important as those questions are, I think they flow downstream from how we view ourselves as residents of a foreign empire. I want us to untangle our political identity from the kingdom of Babylon and situate it in the kingdom of God, which itself is a profoundly political community. I want us to distance our hearts from Babylon, *not* because we don't care about the people around us, but precisely because we *do* care—and the best way to care and love and serve is *as* exiles in Babylon who are participating in God's inbreaking rule over the earth. Therefore, I'm more interested in letting the biblical narrative of exile and empire create a lens through which we consider practical political questions in the first place (climate change, gun control, etc.). I want to cultivate an exilic posture from which to address the political questions we face while living under foreign rule.

It's with this primary goal in mind that I want to wrestle with some practical questions, simply to give some examples of how I'm trying to connect the dots between the biblical theology of exile and empire and how I can live faithfully in light of this theology today. I'm under no illusion that everyone will agree with my thoughts below. Some might even find them offensive. Again, these are my own personal, thinking-out-loud reflections, not necessarily gospel truths that I'm commanding everyone to embrace. All I ask is that you weigh my reflections against the biblical narrative we've explored throughout this book.

Abortion and the Church

One of the themes we've touched on is that the main political task of the church is to *be the church*, to embody kingdom values not just in our personal morality but also in our social ethics. "The church does not have a social ethic," writes Stanley Hauerwas, "The church *is* a social ethic."[1] As we approach every ethical question—race relations, immigration, wealth and poverty, sexuality and gender, creation care, and so on—the church should seek to practice the values we hope to see in the world. Yes, the church should address injustices around us, but we should do so *as the church*, as a prophetic community already living out the values we're challenging Babylon to embrace.

Take abortion, for instance. Most Christians are rightly opposed to taking the life of an unborn child, and many rejoiced when the federal legalization of abortion was overturned and power to limit abortions was given back to individual states (*Dobbs v. Jackson*, 2022). Some hailed this Supreme Court decision as a massive victory. They had been fighting for decades to overturn the 1973 *Roe v. Wade* decision, and in their view, *We finally won!*

But did we? Did *we* win?

I think the *Dobbs v. Jackson* ruling was probably a good thing, although as conservative commentator David French has pointed out, "Abortion was more common when it was mostly illegal."[2] In any case, even if we assume that reversing *Roe v. Wade* was a good thing, it's only one small piece of a much greater issue. According to a 2015 Lifeway study, 70 percent of women who get an abortion identify as Christian. Of these women, 23 percent are evangelical and 26 percent attend church at least once a week.[3] Many women who get an abortion probably agree with their Christian peers that abortion isn't morally right.

So why do they do it? Why do they get an abortion?

Every case is different, and I don't claim to know the hearts and minds of women who have had to process such an incredibly difficult decision. But according to Lifeway's study, it seems that the culture of the church had something to do with some of these women's decisions: "2 in 3 women who've had an abortion say church members judge single women who are pregnant (65%) and are more likely to gossip about a woman considering abortion than help her understand her options (64%)."[4] This kind of culture would certainly add motivation to *not* have a child as an unmarried woman.

Furthermore, nearly half of women who've had an abortion say that their "pastor's teachings on forgiveness don't seem to apply to terminated pregnancies," and only 42 percent "say pastors teach God is willing to forgive past abortion." Women with unwanted pregnancies, then, are damned if they do and damned if they don't. If they carry the child to term, they're ridiculed for having sex outside of marriage. If they have an abortion, they're forever excluded from God's grace. It's no shock, then, that "only 7% of women who had abortions said they directly spoke with someone in their church about their decision."[5]

Even if overturning *Roe v. Wade* was a good thing for the unborn, I hesitate to celebrate it as a huge win, since many of our churches are still not hospitable and forgiving places for women with unwanted pregnancies. (And I haven't even mentioned the many other socioeconomic issues that can contribute to a woman's decision to have an abortion.) Could it be that, in our fight to change Babylon's abortion laws, we've still failed to embody the kind of *polis* where women don't feel like an abortion is their only option? Rather than ignoring this church problem to celebrate a Babylonian law, I suggest we embrace a holistic ethic that includes not only sexual morality but also grace, forgiveness, and care for the unborn and their mothers.

Exiles and Political Parties

It's natural that Christians will resonate with some partisan values more than others. I resonate with some messages promoted by the Democratic Party; the same goes for the Republican Party. But I refuse to give any kind of loyalty or allegiance to either party. As a Christian whose citizenship is in God's global kingdom, I can't give my loyalty to any earthly kingdom or to a certain party trying to rule that kingdom.

Loyalty to one party nearly always requires you to be *against* the other party. Such an "us versus them" perspective will most likely suck you into a tribalistic battle God never called you to fight. It's one thing to look at each party from a distance and resonate with certain values they (claim to) promote. But when you give your loyalty to a particular party, you begin to view the world through the lens they've created for you. Make no mistake: political tribes aren't just after your vote; they're after your heart. And they are very good at making disciples.

I felt this in my own life, growing up in my Republican-only context. I quickly absorbed all the values of the Right: pro-military, pro-guns, anti-abortion, pro-death-penalty, anti-feminism, anti-welfare. Any concern for the environment would tag you as the worst possible thing: a liberal. There was little wiggle room to embrace some of these values while rejecting others—you weren't supposed to be against abortion *and* the death penalty. The political right handed me a complete, prepacked ethic. And though I was told it was biblical, I don't think it had been thoroughly washed through Scripture.

I see the same thing among Democrats: pro-choice, anti-guns, pro-gay-marriage, pro-universal-health-care, pro-LGBTQ-rights, anti-anything-Donald-Trump-has-ever-said-in-his-entire-life. Partisan allegiance creates a kind of in-group pressure to toe the party line in every way and prevents you from celebrating something Republicans might value, even if that particular value resonates with the way of Jesus.

I think we need to be extremely cautious about the effects this kind of groupthink has on the way we see the world. When a group demands our allegiance to their way of thinking, this hinders our ability to embrace Christ's upside-down ethic.

Plus, the United States is an empire (or at least, empire-like) that runs on Babylonian power. It embodies the kind of power dynamics that Jesus overturned when he said, "The rulers of the Gentiles lord it over them, and their high officials exercise authority over them. Not so with you." In Christ's kingdom, "whoever wants to become great among you must be your servant" (Matt. 20:25–26). As Christians assess which party they think better reflects Christian values, the way both parties pursue power often goes unnoticed.

Exiles don't try to get ahead by destroying our enemies; instead, we are called to love them. True leadership is marked by humility, kindness, repentance, and self-giving love. Christians should feel nauseated, for instance, when we listen to partisan rhetoric where one side of the political aisle dehumanizes the other. This is a sickening violation of one of the most basic Christian values, that all people are created in God's image. Until one party starts washing the feet of the other, we should pity their silly quest for power, not get sucked into it.

Whatever resonance we may have with certain values (allegedly) promoted by a political party, that resonance must be rooted in the perspective of exiles belonging to a kingdom built on sacrifice and enemy love.

Pledging Allegiance to Babylon

I recited the Pledge of Allegiance for most of my Christian life. I never questioned it. I did it without reservation. As I reflect on why I used to do it, my reasons were always social and cultural; it's what good Americans do. My reasons for pledging were never theological, as if pledging allegiance to my earthly kingdom were an outflow of my faith in a Lamb crucified by the state for treason.

But several years ago, I stopped. I no longer pledge my allegiance to the nation that I'm living in. And to be consistent, I don't look down on my African, Asian, or Middle Eastern brothers and sisters in Christ who also find it hard to pledge allegiance to Zimbabwe, China, Syria, or wherever.

We are to submit to governing authorities and obey the government's laws as long as they don't conflict with the way of Christ. But *allegiance* is a strong term. It has religious connotations and conveys a kind of loyalty that's reserved for Christ alone.

Christians are to be good citizens by being subversive citizens, political prophets, strangers and foreigners who "[turn] the world upside down" by "acting contrary to Caesar's decrees, saying that there is another king—Jesus" (Acts 17:6–7 CSB). The Christian proclamation that Jesus is King is an inherent political protest. It's a declaration that all other rulers and empires are unworthy of our allegiance.

The Pledge of Allegiance isn't just religious; it's liturgical. Repeating it over and over shapes both heart and mind, and it fosters a kind of identity and commitment that I can't give to the country of my sojourn. For readers raised in the United States, try finishing this: "I pledge allegiance to the flag of the ..."

My guess is you were able to finish the pledge without even thinking about it. I haven't publicly recited it in years, and I can still rattle it off in my head. It's so etched into our bones that we can't *not* recite it.

Now let's recite the Apostles' Creed. I'll get us started: "I believe in God, the Father Almighty, Creator of heaven and earth ..."

Were you able to finish it? Unfortunately, I can't either. I've pledged my allegiance to Babylon more than a thousand times, but I still can't recite a famous early-church pledge to Christ. Or how about the Nicene Creed? Or any summary of the Christian faith? Or can you recite the Ten Commandments? I wonder if Christians are being slowly cooked in the narrative of empire without even realizing it.

For theological reasons, then, I simply cannot pledge my allegiance to the state. I know some of you disagree. This is a touchy issue, for sure. My simple challenge is this: If you still think you should recite the Pledge of Allegiance, you should have robust theological reasons for doing so. Don't just do it because everyone else is or because it's what we've always done.

Turn Off Babylon's News

I believe that one of the greatest threats to Christian discipleship in recent years has been the Christian consumption of mainstream news. I'm not talking about simply staying informed about worldly affairs. I'm talking about the steady drip of partisan propaganda steering our allegiance away from Christ and toward a political party.

Traditional news sources are vying for attention. The more clicks, the more ad revenue. How do you get clicks? By provoking fear and making people angry. When the fires of anger and fear are stoked, people stay tuned in. They keep watching and clicking and yelling and screaming and being used as sources of revenue like products in a market. Put simply, most news outlets aren't just trying to keep you informed. They're after your heart and your wallet by powerful forms of discipleship.[6] Just ask yourself: *After watching an hour of, say, CNN or Fox News, am I* more *or* less *motivated to love my neighbor on the other side of the political aisle?* If the answer is "less," then this is a profound discipleship problem.

I'll admit, I sometimes break my own rule. I watch left- or right-leaning news outlets to get a feel for what each side is saying, and I'm stunned at how quickly my heart is co-opted into hating rather than loving my neighbors and enemies.[7] When I listen to right-wing commentators, my love for people on the left is snuffed out—even if they're Christians. The same is true when I absorb left-wing media. I find myself clicking and clicking while anger and fear suffocate my love for other people. Make no mistake—this is a massive hindrance to following Jesus, who called us to love our neighbors and enemies.

I think it's important to stay informed. I'm only suggesting that Christians should be vigilant about screening the means by which we do so.[8] Most news outlets—even outlets that call themselves

Christian—aren't just reporting the facts. They're promoting a narrative about one side of the political aisle being way worse than the other. It's a power move. They want us on their team, but Christians have already been bought by another team.

We should also recognize that the human heart can handle only so much information, especially about various injustices and tragedies in the world. It's good to be aware of evil and suffering in the world, particularly for those of us living relatively comfortable middle-class lives. But there is a tipping point. When we consume more and more information about evil and suffering, we become overwhelmed and incapacitated. We might rattle off some angry posts on social media, but we end up not doing anything meaningful to address injustice.

Rather than living in an online world through social media or news sites, we should focus on the embodied people in the local space where God has placed us. You probably won't be able to do much about a mass shooting halfway across the country. Spending time responding to Facebook posts about gun laws or gun rights will make little or no difference. But if you look up from your phone and dig into the lives of people around you, you'll discover a lot of pain and suffering that you actually can do something about—pain and suffering that didn't make it into the news.

Christ Reigns in November

Every other November is election season (either presidential or midterm) in the United States. At the time of writing, the US is coming up on one of the most heated presidential elections in decades. Many Christian voters will lose their minds if their preferred candidate doesn't get elected. And this concerns me. I fear that people whose emotions are running high this November might be investing too much hope in Babylon.

But if we embrace our exilic identity, then no matter which Babylonian leader gets elected, Christ is still King and his kingdom will continue to fill his creation by the power of love and sacrifice. This perspective doesn't mean we don't care about justice and evil. It just means we don't trust the beast (empire) to destroy the dragon (Satan). The most effective and faithful way to address evil and establish justice is through the church *being the church*, embodying the kind of *polis* we hope to see in the world. We can do this no matter who's living in the White House.

We can therefore have a kind of theological confidence no matter who Babylon decides its next leader will be. The leader of Babylon is still leading Babylon—and the Leader of God's kingdom hasn't changed. I think it's natural to have an opinion about which Babylonian leader might be better at ruling Babylon, but our opinion on the matter should be *as exiles* not as *Babylonians*. The Jewish exiles probably thought Nebuchadnezzar (who destroyed the temple) was worse than Cyrus (who helped rebuild it). But at the end of the day, the exiles' mission as "a kingdom of priests and a holy nation" (Ex. 19:6) carried on no matter who was ruling the empire. And investing too much hope in Babylon's leaders—and freaking out about people who put their hope in different Babylonian leaders—not only hinders our kingdom mission but could amount to idolatry.

If we embrace our exilic identity, then no matter which Babylonian leader gets elected, Christ is still King and his kingdom will continue to fill his creation by the power of love and sacrifice.

Now, some say that only privileged people can be disinterested in election outcomes while nonprivileged people are deeply affected when bad leaders occupy the White House. I think this is a very important point to consider. To be clear, I'm not saying that real people aren't affected by real decisions made in the White House. I'm more than eager to echo the cry of the prophets who lamented when the nations did evil and denounced leaders who abused their power. I'm just suspicious about putting faith in one side of the Babylonian aisle to institute the kind of justice we want to see in the world. (I also think we should be more skeptical of media propaganda that reinforces doomsday-type messages about what will happen if the "other party" gets elected.) When the prophets of old lamented the evil of the nations, they didn't put their faith in a "good" national leader to confront a "bad" one; rather, they put their faith in God's kingdom and his power to judge evil empires.

Again, I think there is a place for the church to address societal injustices and even call on Babylon to change unjust laws, as the abolitionists and civil rights movement did. But this should be an expression of our allegiance to Christ, not a replacement of it. And when the church divides over which Babylonian leader is best, this too is a kind of evil that we should be deeply concerned about.

In short, our confidence in certain Babylonian leaders and tribes should be tempered by a kind of cool theological suspicion derived from our ultimate confession: *No king but Christ.*

Read the Bible Politically

As exiles, we should form our views on immigration, creation care, social justice, sexuality, and gender from the Bible. Of course, all Christians will say they do this. But saying is one thing; doing is another.

I'll never forget preaching a sermon about refugees at a church in Boise, Idaho, where I live. Boise is a major refugee resettlement city in the US, and several years ago, discussions had flared up in our local churches as a result of news stories involving Donald Trump and refugees. When I was asked to preach one Sunday, I told the pastor I wanted to give an overview of what the Bible says about refugees. He enthusiastically agreed that this was needed.

My sermon wasn't partisan; it wasn't even "political" in the popular sense of the term. It wasn't dogmatic or divisive. I simply surveyed what the Bible says about immigrants, foreigners, and refugees and drew a rather vanilla conclusion: God seems to care about immigrants and refugees, and so should we. I didn't say anything related to the government's immigration policies or whether the US should build walls around its borders or tear them down. I stayed clear of Babylon's policy debates. I simply surveyed the Bible to cultivate a kingdom-of-Christ perspective on the issue, and I probably quoted more passages of Scripture than I ever have in a sermon before.

The message was generally well received, but a few people hated it. They said it was the worst sermon they'd ever heard. Why? They thought it was too "political." They said I was pushing some liberal agenda.

> **The most effective and faithful way to address evil and establish justice is through the church *being the church*, embodying the kind of *polis* we hope to see in the world.**

My sermon might have been terrible. I don't claim to be a good preacher. But too political? Liberal agenda? I fear that these listeners' theological categories had been hijacked by certain partisan news outlets that brainwashed them into thinking any pro-immigrant, pro-refugee talk must be liberal.

Since the Bible verses I quoted didn't fit their partisan narrative, these Bible verses were considered … unbiblical.

This is just one story, but I've seen this way of approaching political questions to be pervasive in the church. Our opinions on various cultural topics have been shaped by partisan perspectives, and when we hear something that goes against our opinions, we consider it wrong instead of asking, "Is it biblical?" Exiles should *begin* with the Bible and *then* let the Bible shape our perspective on this or that cultural issue, regardless of whether it lines up with a certain political party.

Of course, Christians will come to different conclusions on what the Bible actually says about immigration, sexuality, creation care, and other political topics. I'm under no illusion that every exile just needs to read the Bible and then we'll all be on the same page and live happily ever after. I'm simply saying that we should have good-faith discussions about what the Bible says about these things, rather than forming our views from modern political discussions and *then* taking these back to the Bible to find verses to support them.

Practice Enemy Love

> You have heard that it was said, *"Love your neighbor and hate your enemy."* But I tell you, love your enemies and pray for those who persecute you. (Matt. 5:43–44)

Christ's command to love our enemies became the early church's most distinguishing feature. You can find virtually all other Christian values promoted in other religious systems. But enemy love sets Christianity apart from the rest. "If you love those who love you," Christ said, "what are you doing out of the ordinary?" (vv. 46–47 CSB). In fact, Matthew 5:44 was *the* most quoted verse in the first three hundred years of the church.[9] If we are going to be a compelling prophetic witness in society, the church must be known for its love for enemies.

Anecdotally, I don't think we are. We live in an increasingly polarized society, and the church looks no different. We bicker and badger, mock and make fun of people who believe differently from us—especially on social media. The same outrage that permeates society fills our pews and our phones. It's not shocking when Babylon does this. The empire thinks they gain power by destroying their enemies, so of course the Left will blast the Right and the Right will blast the Left. But when the church looks no different—*and divides along the same left/right Babylonian lines*—then Satan must be doubled over laughing.

During the COVID-19 pandemic, for instance, we saw whole churches divide over things like whether we should wear masks. I get that there were a lot of unknowns during the pandemic; I don't want to downplay the seriousness of the virus and the complicated responses to it. But wouldn't this have been the best time to come together as a church? In the face of a global pandemic? To listen to one another, show respect and honor, and humanize our fellow blood-bought image bearers—even if we disagreed over matters like mask wearing?

It's a sad day when the unity of the church, created by the death and resurrection of our King, can be torn apart by a six-inch mask.

What's more, the issue of masks was clearly politicized by both sides of the aisle. Trump wouldn't wear a mask, so the Left would wear two. (I wonder what would have happened if *Trump* had actually worn two masks. Would the Left have worn any?) The whole thing turned into another power game between the Left and the Right—and many Christians followed suit. They demonstrated stronger devotion to their political tribe than to their church.

If we can't love and honor a brother or sister in Christ because he or she wears or doesn't wear a mask, how are we going to take on "the cosmic powers of this darkness, against evil, spiritual forces in the heavens" (Eph. 6:12 CSB)—the *real* enemy?

Believing that the crucified and resurrected Lamb rules the universe should be radical enough to bind the church together as citizens of an upside-down kingdom that's conquering the world through sacrificial love.

Conclusion

All my thoughts above are, of course, debated and disruptive, and I certainly don't think every reader will agree with how I'm thinking through certain issues. My ultimate goal in this book, though, is that Christians today would let the scriptural theme of exile shape their political identity. Viewing ourselves as exiles in the shadow of empire should cultivate a kind of theological wedge between our allegiance to Christ and our commitment to the nation we're living in. Christians will continue to debate various political issues. But believing that the crucified and resurrected Lamb rules the universe should be radical enough to bind the church together as citizens of an upside-down kingdom that's conquering the world through sacrificial love.

Against the backdrop of Israel's anti-nation-like nation, their ensuing exile, Jesus' upside-down kingdom, Paul's counter-imperial gospel, Peter's exilic community, and John's revelation that all empires are beasts co-opted by Satan and defeated by a sacrificial Lamb—the church is called to embrace its exile, embody a cruciform life, and show the world what it means to flourish as a community of image bearers in God's creation.

NOTES

Chapter 1: The Politics of Church

1. See Young-Ho Park, *Paul's Ekklesia as a Civic Assembly: Understanding the People of God in Their Politico-Social World* (Tübingen: Mohr Siebeck, 2015).

2. C. W. Blackwell, "The Assembly," in *Demos: Classical Athenian Democracy*, ed. C. W. Blackwell (A. Mahoney and R. Scaife, eds., *The Stoa: A Consortium for Electronic Publication in the Humanities* edition of March 26, 2003), 1.

3. Blackwell, "The Assembly," 1.

4. Blackwell, "The Assembly," 1.

5. See Park, *Paul's Ekklesia as a Civic Assembly*, 5–61. One of the main differences is that the Greek *ekklēsia* was more democratically ruled, while in the Roman world it was much more oligarchical, with the wealthy holding the power.

6. See Dio Chrysostom, *Orationes* 31, 34, 40, 43; Plutarch, *Moralia* 798–99, 813D, 815C–D; Aeschines, *Against Timarchus* 22–23.

7. See Dinarchus, *Against Aristogiton* 14, 16; Aristophanes, *Acharnenses* 44. See also Aeschines, *Against Timarchus* 22–23; cf. the discussion in Andrew D. Clarke, *Serve the Community of the Church: Christians as Leaders and Ministers* (Grand Rapids, MI: Eerdmans, 2000), 21–22.

8. Paul and others didn't just choose *ekklēsia* since *synagōgē* was already taken by the Jews; "the word *synagōgē* was not only utilized for Jewish groups but was also very frequently used for small groups, including voluntary associations" (Park, *Paul's Ekklesia as a Civic Assembly*, 61).

9. See Clarke, *Serve the Community of the Church*, 19–25.

10. "Each Graeco-Roman city prospered or declined under the perceived patronage or guardianship of its gods or goddesses" (Clarke, *Serve the Community of the Church*, 19).

11. Stanley Hauerwas and William H. Willimon, *Resident Aliens: Life in the Christian Colony*, rev. ed. (Nashville, TN: Abingdon, 2014), 38.

12. For a good introduction to political theology, see Elizabeth Phillips, *Political Theology: A Guide for the Perplexed* (London: T&T Clark, 2012).

13. William T. Cavanaugh and Peter Scott, introduction to *The Blackwell Companion to Political Theology*, ed. Peter Scott and William T. Cavanaugh (Oxford: Blackwell, 2004), 1.

14. Timothy G. Gombis, "The Political Vision of the Apostle to the Nations," in *Christian Political Witness*, ed. George Kalantzis and Gregory W. Lee (Downers Grove, IL: IVP Academic, 2014), 75–76.

15. Lee Camp says it like this: "[A politic is] an all-encompassing manner of communal life that grapples with all the questions the classical art of politics has always asked: How do we live together? How do we deal with offenses? How do we deal with money? How do we deal with enemies and violence? How do we arrange marriage and families and social structures? How is authority mediated, employed, ordered? How do we rightfully order passions and appetites? And much more besides, but most especially add these: Where is human history headed? What does it mean to be human? And what does it look like to live in a rightly ordered human community that engenders flourishing, justice, and the peace of God?" (*Scandalous Witness: A Little Political Manifesto for Christians* [Grand Rapids, MI: Eerdmans, 2020], 4).

16. See Zechariah 2:7; 1 Peter 5:13; and Revelation 17–18, where *Babel* or *Babylon* (it's the same word in the Hebrew) "becomes a trope for a particular configuration of political power" (Peter J. Leithart, *Between Babel and Beast: America and Empires in Biblical Perspective* [Eugene, OR: Cascade Books, 2012], 153n1). The Bible does the same thing with other cities and nations, like Sodom (Deut. 29:23; Isa. 1:9–10; Ezek. 16:46–47) and Egypt (Rev. 11:8).

17. Leithart, *Between Babel and Beast*, 154–55n1 (emphasis mine).

18. The biblical word used to describe these empires is "kingdom" (*malchut* in the Hebrew and *basileia* in the Greek). *Kingdom* is a broader term than *empire*, as it can include empires but can also refer to nations that aren't empires according to Leithart's definition above.

19. Samir Puri, *The Shadows of Empire: How Imperial History Shapes Our World* (New York: Pegasus Books, 2021), 27.

Chapter 2: Israel's Upside-Down Kingdom

1. Throughout this chapter and the next, when I talk about Israel being different, I have in mind how God intended Israel to live, not its actual behavior, which often fell short of God's design.

2. Cf. Deut. 4:32–34; Christopher J. H. Wright, *Old Testament Ethics for the People of God* (Downers Grove, IL: IVP Academic, 2004), 52.

3. Even the way the Israelites approached writing and literacy went against the grain of the hierarchical class distinctions evident in other Near Eastern cultures. See the fascinating discussion in Joshua A. Berman, *Created Equal: How the Bible Broke with Ancient Political Thought* (New York: Oxford University Press, 2008), 109–33.

4. "The ancient Near East considered kingship the very basis of civilization. Only savages could live without a king" (Henri Frankfort, *Kingship and the Gods: A Study of Ancient Near Eastern Religion as the Integration of Society and Nature* [Chicago: University of Chicago Press, 1978], 3). See also John Day, ed., *King and Messiah in Israel and the Ancient Near East: Proceedings of the Oxford Old Testament Seminar* (London: Bloomsbury, 2013).

5. Berman, *Created Equal*, 53.

6. Patricia Dutcher-Walls, "The Circumscription of the King: Deuteronomy 17:16–17 in Its Ancient Social Context," *Journal of Biblical Literature* 121, no. 4 (2002): 604.

7. "As a theocratic state, Israel's only true king was the Lord, and there was a sense in which it would seem presumptuous for a man to assume the title" (Peter C. Craigie, *The Book of Deuteronomy* [Grand Rapids, MI: Eerdmans, 1976], 253).

8. Patrick Miller writes, "The law of the king places upon that figure the obligations incumbent upon every Israelite. In that sense, Deuteronomy's primary concern was that the king *be the model*

Israelite" (Patrick D. Miller, *Deuteronomy* [Louisville, KY: John Knox, 1990], 148–49), (emphasis mine).

9. "Alone among the literary works of the ancient Near East, the Hebrew Bible maintains that the law is of divine origin" (Berman, *Created Equal*, 59).

10. *Oxford English Dictionary*, s.v. "militarism," OED.com, accessed August 3, 2023.

11. Craigie, *Book of Deuteronomy*, 275.

12. Douglas K. Stuart, "The Old Testament Context of David's Costly Flirtation with Empire-Building," in *Empire in the New Testament*, ed. Stanley E. Porter and Cynthia Long Westfall (Eugene, OR: Pickwick, 2011), 35–36.

13. See Josh. 11:6, 9; 2 Sam. 8:4; cf. Mic. 5:10.

14. Cited in Erika Bleibtreu, "Grisly Assyrian Record of Torture and Death," *Biblical Archaeology Review* 17, no. 1 (1991): 51–61, 75.

15. Norman K. Gottwald, *The Tribes of Yahweh: A Sociology of the Religion of Liberated Israel, 1250–1050 BCE* (Sheffield, UK: Sheffield Academic, 1999), 212.

16. "In the Canaanite city-states the king owned all the land and there were feudal arrangements with those who lived and worked on it as tax-paying tenant peasants. In Israel the land was divided up as widely as possible into multiple ownership by extended families" (Wright, *Old Testament Ethics*, 55–56; cf. 89).

17. See Berman, *Created Equal*, 93.

18. Wright, *Old Testament Ethics*, 157. See also Gottwald, *Tribes of Yahweh*, 212–14, 391–94.

19. See Berman, *Created Equal*, 90.

20. See Num. 18:8–32; Deut. 14:27; 18:3–5. Priests and Levites "were given specifically designated residential holdings," but they "could not amass additional holdings" and "could not hold agricultural lands" (Berman, *Created Equal*, 93).

21. Wright, *Old Testament Ethics*, 57.

22. See Berman, *Created Equal*, 92–96.

23. See Berman, *Created Equal*, 96; cf. I. Mendelsohn, "Slavery in the Ancient Near East," *The Biblical Archaeologist* 9, no. 4 (1946): 79–80, who lists rates as high as 80 percent.

24. See Ex. 22:25; Lev. 25:35–37; Deut. 23:20.

25. See Ex. 21:2–6; Lev. 25:39–54; Deut. 15:12–18. See also Berman, *Created Equal*, 99.

26. E.g., Isa. 3:14–15; Ezek. 16:49; 22:29; Amos 2:6–7; 4:1; Mic. 2:1–2.

27. Nilay Saiya, *The Global Politics of Jesus: A Christian Case for Church-State Separation* (New York: Oxford University Press, 2022), 20.

28. "It is clear that in the New Kingdom (c. 1550–1070 B.C.E.) the priesthood controlled an immense amount of land" (Berman, *Created Equal*, 93).

29. In Mesopotamia, the king would often appoint his own relatives to the priesthood (see Leopold Sabourin, *Priesthood: A Comparative Study* [Leiden: Brill, 1973], 65).

30. Berman, *Created Equal*, 71.

31. If we had more space, we could look at other countercultural values that shaped Israel's society, such as its tribal leadership and other more sensitive issues surrounding women and slaves. As other scholars have shown, even the treatment of women and slaves in the Old

Testament would have been viewed as countercultural. While falling short of a full application of Genesis 1:27, where women are completely equal to men and slavery is nonexistent, the Old Testament still stands out as a significant improvement against the backdrop of other Near Eastern societies. On tribal leadership, see Berman, *Created Equal*, 73–78. Many scholars have examined women and slavery in the Old Testament. For an accessible resource with an extensive bibliography, see Paul Copan, *Is God a Moral Monster? Making Sense of the Old Testament God* (Grand Rapids, MI: Baker Books, 2011).

32. See John 8:12; Acts 13:47; 26:23; 1 Pet. 2:9.

33. Daniel L. Smith-Christopher, *The Religion of the Landless: The Social Context of the Babylonian Exile* (Eugene, OR: Wipf and Stock, 2015), 213 (emphasis mine).

Chapter 3: Exiled to Babylon

1. See Peter J. Leithart, *Between Babel and Beast: America and Empires in Biblical Perspective* (Eugene, OR: Cascade Books, 2012), 4–8; John H. Yoder, "See How They Go with Their Face to the Sun," in John H. Yoder, *For the Nations: Essays Evangelical and Public* (Grand Rapids, MI: Eerdmans, 1997), 61–63.

2. Leithart, *Between Babel and Beast*, 4.

3. Leithart, *Between Babel and Beast*, 5.

4. Yoder, "See How They Go," 62–63.

5. J. Richard Middleton, *The Liberating Image: The* Imago Dei *in Genesis 1* (Grand Rapids, MI: Brazos, 2005), 224.

6. The Assyrian king Ashurbanipal II, for instance, "made the totality of all peoples speak one speech," and Sargon II boasted, "Populations of the four world quarters with strange tongues and incompatible

speech ... whom I had taken as booty at the command of Asshur my lord by the might of my scepter, I caused to accept a single voice" (cited in Middleton, *Liberating Image*, 224).

7. Middleton, *Liberating Image*, 226. Some say that the tower itself was a religious shrine, perhaps an ancient ziggurat. But as Middleton points out, the word for "tower" (Hebrew: *migdal*) is often used of military fortresses throughout the Old Testament (e.g., Judg. 8:9, 17; 9:46–52; Ps. 48:12; Isa. 2:15; Ezek. 26:9); see *Liberating Image*, 223.

8. Middleton, *Liberating Image*, 223. See, e.g., Isa. 14:3–23 and Jer. 51.

9. "'Ur of the Chaldeans,' a site considerably south of Babylon ... is the home of Terah's family (11:28, 31; cf. 15:7; Neh. 9:7). Although some have attributed this site to northern Mesopotamia, it is widely held that Ur is in the southern region of Babylonia (modern Tell el-Muqayyar)" (Kenneth A. Mathews, *Genesis 1–11:26* [Nashville, TN: Broadman & Holman, 1996], 476).

10. Quite literally in the case of Eli, who became so obese that he broke his neck when he fell out of his chair (1 Sam. 4:18; cf. the abuse of priestly power in 1 Sam. 2:12–17).

11. Horrors like these are expressed in vivid detail throughout the book of Lamentations.

12. See Daniel L. Smith-Christopher, *The Religion of the Landless: The Social Context of the Babylonian Exile* (Eugene, OR: Wipf and Stock, 2015), 26–41.

13. This is the view of most scholars. However, some see the conditions of exile as much more oppressive. At the very least, I think it's safe to say that the social status and overall quality of life for the Jewish exiles were mixed (see Smith-Christopher, *Religion of the Landless*, 35–41).

14. See Daniel I. Block, *The Book of Ezekiel: Chapters 1–24* (Grand Rapids, MI: Eerdmans, 1997), 6–7.

15. Jon L. Berquist, "Resistance and Accommodation in the Persian Empire," in *In the Shadow of Empire: Reclaiming the Bible as a History of Faithful Resistance*, ed. Richard A. Horsley (Louisville, KY: Westminster John Knox, 2008), 44.

16. "Among the relevant aspects of the Babylonian Exile community was the fact that it was not only a minority, but it was a *conquered* minority, *under domination*" (Smith-Christopher, *Religion of the Landless*, 60), (emphasis mine).

17. James K. A. Smith points out that the line between religion and politics is just as blurry today; see his *Awaiting the King: Reforming Public Theology*, Cultural Liturgies, vol. 3 (Grand Rapids, MI: Baker, 2017), 19–52.

18. Smith-Christopher, *Religion of the Landless*, 57–58 (emphasis original).

19. Other prophets were more explicitly critical of Babylon. Isaiah 40–55, for instance, gives a very negative picture of Babylon (42:18–25; 46:8–12; 47:1–15).

20. The events of Jeremiah 28–29, including Hananiah's and Jeremiah's conflicting prophecies about the end of exile, occurred in 594 BC. This was just three years after the second wave of exile in 597 BC (the first was in 605 BC) and shortly before the last wave of exile and destruction of the temple in 586 BC.

21. Smith-Christopher, *Religion of the Landless*, 133.

22. Smith-Christopher, *Religion of the Landless*, 135.

23. See Mic. 3:5; Zech. 8:12; Mal. 2:5.

24. Joseph P. Healey, "Peace: Old Testament," in *The Anchor Bible Dictionary*, ed. David Noel Freedman, vol. 5, *O–Sh* (New York: Doubleday, 1992), 207.

25. The identities of the four empires in Daniel are disputed. Josephus and other early Jewish writers agree with the four I mention here (see Josephus, *Ant.* 10.10.4; cf. 4 Ezra 12:10–16). Some modern scholars, however, don't believe the fourth beast is Rome; rather, they view the four kingdoms as Babylon, Media, Persia, and Greece (see, e.g., John J. Collins, *Daniel: A Commentary on the Book of Daniel*, ed. Frank Moore Cross [Minneapolis: Fortress, 1993], 166–70).

26. Some say that Daniel 1–6 gives a very different political perspective from chapters 7–12. The first half portrays political rulers quite positively, while the latter half is much more critical and therefore has "a political stance diametrically opposed to that implied in the tales" of Daniel 1–6 (Collins, *Daniel*, 52). Certainly, there's a tension, but this same tension runs throughout Scripture. Earthly empires are beasts, but God's people are to submit to their rule since they trust God's ultimate rule over human affairs.

27. Yoder, "See How They Go," 71.

28. Smith-Christopher, *Religion of the Landless*, 215.

29. Berquist, "Resistance and Accommodation," 56.

30. "We see that in some writings from the postexilic period, exile no longer signifies a historical event completed in the past but, instead, a concept describing the ongoing present condition.... Thus, in the course of time, exile came to be understood not merely as a historical event in the past but as an existential mode of being" (Adele Berlin, "The Exile: Biblical Ideology and Its Postmodern Ideological Interpretation," in *Literary Construction of Identity in the Ancient World: Proceedings of the Conference Literary Fiction and the*

Construction of Identity in Ancient Literatures; Options and Limits of Modern Literary Approaches in the Exegesis of Ancient Texts Heidelberg, July 10–13, 2006, ed. Hanna Liss and Manfred Oeming [Winona Lake, IN: Eisenbrauns, 2010], 350–51).

31. See Michael A. Knibb, "The Exile in the Literature of the Intertestamental Period," *Heythrop Journal* 27, no. 3 (1976): 253–72.

32. See 1 Pet. 1:1; 2:11; 5:13; Heb. 11:9–10, 13, 15–16; Rev. 14:8; 17:5; 18:2. See also 2 Baruch 11:1–2; 67:7; 2 Esdras 3:1–2, 28; Sib. Or. 5.143, 155–61; and, for the early church, e.g., Tertullian, *Against Marcion* 3.13; Augustine, *City of God* 18.22.

33. Smith-Christopher, *Religion of the Landless*, 214.

34. Smith-Christopher, *Religion of the Landless*, 213 (emphasis mine).

35. See Richard A. Horsley, *Bandits, Prophets, and Messiahs: Popular Movements in the Time of Jesus* (Harrisburg, PA: Trinity, 1999).

36. See N. T. Wright, *The New Testament and the People of God* (Minneapolis: Fortress, 1992), 181–203.

Chapter 4: Jesus, the New Israel, and the Kingdom Not of This World

1. Scot McKnight, *"Extra Ecclesiam Nullum Regnum*: The Politics of Jesus," in *Christian Political Witness*, ed. George Kalantzis and Gregory W. Lee (Downers Grove, IL: IVP Academic, 2014), 59 (emphasis mine).

2. See Luke 1:46–55; cf. 1 Sam. 2:1–10.

3. See Dale C. Allison, *The Sermon on the Mount: Inspiring the Moral Imagination* (New York: Herder & Herder, 1999), 17–19.

4. Warren Carter, *What Are They Saying about Matthew's Sermon on the Mount?* (Mahwah, NJ: Paulist, 1994), 21.

5. Jonathan Sgalambro, "The Upside Down Kingdom: An Introduction to the Sermon on the Mount," Redeemer Fellowship, October 2, 2019, www.redeemernj.com/pastorsblog/post/the-upside -down-kingdom-an-introduction-to-the-sermon-on-the-mount.

6. Matthew's preferred phrase "kingdom of *heaven*" doesn't refer to some place in the sky where believers will go when they die; rather, the term *heaven* was often used in Judaism as a synonym for "God's presence." Similarly, some English versions of Luke 17:21 have Jesus saying "the kingdom of God is *within you*" (NKJV), which suggests some kind of private, internal kingdom where Christ reigns over our hearts. But this is now widely recognized as a mistranslation of the Greek word *entos*, which should be rendered "in your midst" (NIV) or "among you" (NLT).

7. Timothy G. Gombis, "The Political Vision of the Apostle to the Nations," in *Christian Political Witness*, ed. George Kalantzis and Gregory W. Lee (Downers Grove, IL: IVP Academic, 2014), 75.

8. Warren Carter, *The Roman Empire and the New Testament: An Essential Guide* (Nashville, TN: Abingdon, 2006), 31.

9. See Warren Carter, "Matthew and Empire," in *Empire in the New Testament*, ed. Stanley E. Porter and Cynthia Long Westfall (Eugene, OR: Pickwick, 2011), 114–15.

10. Carter, "Matthew and Empire," 114.

11. Keith Simon, "Paid in Full: Why The Crossing Erased $43 Million in Missouri Medical Debt," The Crossing, August 23, 2019, https://info.thecrossingchurch.com/blog/paid-in-full-why-the-crossing -erased-43-million-in-missouri-medical-debt.

12. See Benjamin C. Nelson, "The Crossing Helps Relieve $43 Million of Medical Debt," *Macon County Home Press*, September 11, 2019, www.maconhomepress.com/articles/2731/view.

13. Simon, "Paid in Full."

14. Julian, letter to Arsacius, in *The Works of the Emperor Julian*, trans. Wilmer Cave Wright, vol. 3 (London: William Heinemann, 1923), 71.

15. Stanley Hauerwas and William H. Willimon, *Resident Aliens: Life in the Christian Colony*, rev. ed. (Nashville, TN: Abingdon, 2014), 41.

Chapter 5: Jesus and the Subversion of Empire

1. See Warren Carter, "Matthew and Empire," in *Empire in the New Testament*, ed. Stanley E. Porter and Cynthia Long Westfall (Eugene, OR: Pickwick, 2011), 114.

2. It was Mark Antony and the Roman Senate that gave Herod the Great the title "king of the Jews" in 40 BC: Antony "resolved to have him made king of the Jews" (Josephus, *War* 1.282; cf. 1.388; cf. *Ant.* 14.9; 15.9, 373, 409). See Craig A. Evans, "King Jesus and His Ambassadors: Empire and Luke–Acts," in *Empire in the New Testament*, ed. Stanley E. Porter and Cynthia Long Westfall (Eugene, OR: Pickwick, 2011), 122.

3. Herod murdered Mariamne (one of his wives), her brother, her grandfather, her mother, and his two sons born to Mariamne, which led Caesar Augustus to say, "It is better to be Herod's pig than son" (Macrobius, *Saturnalia* 2.4.11). In case you didn't catch it, pigs are safe around Jews, who don't eat pork.

4 See James S. Jeffers, *The Greco-Roman World of the New Testament Era: Exploring the Background of Early Christianity* (Downers Grove, IL: InterVarsity, 1999), 180–96.

5. "The census is an instrument of imperial rule and domination. Empires count people so that they can tax them to sustain the elite's

exploitative lifestyle" (Warren Carter, *The Roman Empire and the New Testament: An Essential Guide* [Nashville, TN: Abingdon, 2006], 29).

6. See Acts 5:37; Josephus, *War* 2.433; *Ant.* 18.1–10, 23.

7. Bruce W. Winter, *Divine Honours for the Caesars: The First Christians' Responses* (Grand Rapids, MI: Eerdmans, 2015), 37.

8. Patrick Schreiner, *Political Gospel: Public Witness in a Politically Crazy World* (Nashville, TN: B&H, 2022), 43–44.

9. Schreiner, *Political Gospel*, 44.

10. In Daniel, for instance, Michael the archangel waged war against the demonic forces behind the kingdom of Persia before launching an attack on the demonic powers behind Greece (10:12–21; cf. 12:1). See also John 12:31; 14:30; 16:11; 2 Cor. 4:4; Eph. 6:11–12; 1 John 5:19; Rev. 12–13.

11. Carter, *Roman Empire and the New Testament*, 17.

12. See Carter, *Roman Empire and the New Testament*, 5.

13. See Schreiner, *Political Gospel*, 33.

14. See Joseph H. Hellerman, *Embracing Shared Ministry: Power and Status in the Early Church and Why It Matters Today* (Grand Rapids, MI: Kregel, 2013), 66–79; Andrew D. Clarke, *Serve the Community of the Church: Christians as Leaders and Ministers* (Grand Rapids, MI: Eerdmans, 2000), 41–49.

15. Hellerman, *Embracing Shared Ministry*, 67. Andrew Clarke likewise points out that "a post on this *cursus honorum* should be viewed not as a job, but as a social status" (*Serve the Community of the Church*, 41).

16. See Matt. 28:1–10; Mark 16:1–8; Luke 24:1–10; John 20:1–18.

17. Mark 10:31; cf. Matt. 20:16; Mark 9:35; Luke 13:30.

18. Matt. 23:12 NASB; see Luke 14:11; 18:14; cf. Matt. 18:4.

19. See Matt. 22:15–22; Mark 12:13–17; Luke 20:20–26.

20. See especially Scot McKnight, "*Extra Ecclesiam Nullum Regnum*: The Politics of Jesus," in *Christian Political Witness*, ed. George Kalantzis and Gregory W. Lee (Downers Grove, IL: IVP Academic, 2014), 68–71.

21. See N. T. Wright, *The New Testament and the People of God* (Minneapolis: Fortress, 1992), 181–203.

22. Richard Bauckham, *The Bible in Politics: How to Read the Bible Politically*, 2nd ed. (London: SPCK, 2010), 76.

23. "The Jews … said that the Romans built fine bridges simply in order to be able to collect tolls for the use of them!" (Bauckham, *Bible in Politics*, 77).

24. Bauckham, *Bible in Politics*, 76.

25. The first denarii struck by Augustus in 38 BC depicted Julius Caesar and Augustus facing each other with the titles "god Julius" and "son of a god." In a Roman colony in Bithynia and Pontus, coins were struck in 27 BC that said "Julius, god" and, on the reverse, "Augustus, son of a god." In Thessalonica, coins were stamped with a crowned Julius Caesar and the title "god" (see Winter, *Divine Honours*, 64–67).

26. Tom Thatcher, "'I Have Conquered the World': The Death of Jesus and the End of Empire in the Gospel of John," in *Empire in the New Testament*, ed. Stanley E. Porter and Cynthia Long Westfall (Eugene, OR: Pickwick, 2011), 145.

27. Thatcher, "'I Have Conquered the World,'" 147.

28. Quintilian, *Decl.* 274, in *The Lesser Declamations*, trans. and ed. D. R. Shackleton Bailey (Cambridge, MA: Harvard University Press, 2006), 1:259.

29. Cicero, *Rab. Post.* 5.16, in *The Speeches of Cicero*, trans. H. Grose Hodge (London: William Heinemann, 1966), 467.

30. Thatcher, "'I Have Conquered the World,'" 145.

31. John 19:28; cf. vv. 24, 36–37.

32. There was a rumor surrounding the death of Nero that he would return alive at some point, but this resurrection-like myth is an exception that proves the rule.

33. Schreiner, *Political Gospel*, 38.

34. Paul Anleitner (@PaulAnleitner), Twitter, January 25, 2023, 8:55 a.m., https://twitter.com/PaulAnleitner/status/1618276285482160129.

Chapter 6: Paul and the Counter-Imperial Gospel

1. "The Romans wished to believe they stood for order and sobriety in public life," and "undergirding this was a belief that *Romanitas* was superior to other forms of human culture" (David Nystrom, "We Have No King but Caesar: Roman Imperial Ideology and the Imperial Cult," in *Jesus Is Lord, Caesar Is Not: Evaluating Empire in New Testament Studies*, ed. Scot McKnight and Joseph B. Modica [Downers Grove, IL: IVP Academic, 2013], 24–25).

2. As T. W. Hillard and others have shown, there was no singular, monolithic imperial cult but diverse expressions of emperor worship—hence his preference of "imperial cults" rather than "*the* imperial cult" (see "Vespasian's Death-Bed Attitude to His Impending Deification," in *Religion in the Ancient World: New Themes and Approaches*, ed. Matthew Dillon [Amsterdam: Hakkert, 1996], 197–98n33). See also Bruce W. Winter, *Divine Honours for the Caesars: The First Christians' Responses* (Grand Rapids, MI: Eerdmans, 2015), 49.

3. While the evidence is mixed and complicated, it seems that Augustus (reign 27 BC–AD 14) rejected veneration when he was alive but was hailed as a god after he died. His son Tiberius (reign AD 14–37) also seems to have rejected worship early on, but later in his life, he embraced a divine status. Interestingly, Herod the Great built a temple to venerate Augustus (and the goddess Roma) while he was still alive, and Pontius Pilate dedicated a shrine to Tiberius. On the origins of the imperial cult, see Winter, *Divine Honours*, 77–87. From AD 1 to 50, at least ten imperial cult temples were erected throughout Asia Minor (see S. R. F. Price, *Rituals and Power: The Roman Imperial Cult in Asia Minor* [Cambridge: Cambridge University Press, 1985], 59).

4. Greg Carey, "The Book of Revelation as Counter-Imperial Script," in *In the Shadow of Empire: Reclaiming the Bible as a History of Faithful Resistance*, ed. Richard A. Horsley (Louisville, KY: Westminster John Knox, 2008), 163.

5. For instance, it was "politically important … that on significant imperial festivals and holy days, all citizens" show their gratitude to Caesar and allegiance to Rome "by publicly participating in appropriate divine venerations as expressions of their thankfulness for all the imperial blessings they enjoyed and their undying loyalty to Rome" (Winter, *Divine Honours*, 78).

6. E.g., Matt. 14:33; 16:16; 27:54.

7. Nicopolis: *CIG* 1810; Thera: *IG* XII 3.469; Sardis: *Sardis* 7.1, no. 8; Ilium: *IGR* 4.201. For extensive documentation of Paul's shared vocabulary, see Stanley E. Porter, "Paul Confronts Caesar with the Good News," in *Empire in the New Testament*, ed. Stanley E. Porter and Cynthia Long Westfall (Eugene, OR: Pickwick, 2011), 164–96.

8. "Son of the god Augustus" (Laconia: *SEG* 11.922; Cyprus: *OGIS* 583; Lycia: *IGR* 3.721).

9. "Son of Ares" (*CIA* 3.444a); "son of the god Augustus" (*IGR* 4.1094).

10. Nero was often called "Lord Nero," "the one with foreknowledge," "savior," "Zeus the savior," "Zeus the liberator," and "Lord Augustus" (*SIG*³ 814). See Porter, "Paul Confronts Caesar," 173.

11. Ptolemy V was said to have been "god from god and goddess" (*OGIS* 90). Julius Caesar (Greece: *IG* XII 5.557; Lesbos: *Ath. Mitt.* 13 [1888] 61), Augustus (*IGR* 1.1007; *CIG* 1810; *CIG* 778; *IG* XII 3.1104; Galatia: *OGIS* 533; Neapolis: *IGR* 3.137; Cyprus: *IGR* 3.932, 973, 994; *CIG* 2629; Pergamum: *IGR* 4.309, 315, 317, 318), and Caligula (*IGR* 4.67) were all called "god." See Porter, "Paul Confronts Caesar," 166, for references and discussion.

12. Julius Caesar was called "savior and benefactor" in several inscriptions (*IG* VIII.1835; XII.5, 556; *IGR* 9.57, 303, 305; *CIA* 3.428). Augustus was called "savior and benefactor" (*SB* 8897.1; *IGR* 1.901, 1294; 3.426; 4.201, 311–12; *CIA* 3.575–76; *IG* 7.1836; even Philo, *Legat.* 149). Tiberius was called "benefactor of the world" (*SEG* 36 [1986] 1092) and "savior and benefactor" (A. S. Hunt and C. C. Edgar, trans., *Select Papyri* [Cambridge, MA: Harvard University Press, 1963], 2:79, no. 211). Nero was called "savior and benefactor" (*OGI* 668.5; cf. *OGIS* 666.2–7; 814.22–23). Vespasian was called "savior and benefactor" (see Craig A. Evans, "King Jesus and His Ambassadors: Empire and Luke–Acts," in *Empire in the New Testament*, ed. Stanley E. Porter and Cynthia Long Westfall [Eugene, OR: Pickwick, 2011], 127–29).

13. Julius Caesar (*IG* XII 2.165b) and Augustus (*CIA* 3.30; "god," "creator," and "savior": *IGR* 3.546; 4.311).

14. This was one of Julius Caesar's official titles, later assumed by Augustus (Augustus, *Achievements* 10.2) and all emperors of the first three centuries AD (see Andrew D. Clarke, *Serve the Community of*

the Church: Christians as Leaders and Ministers [Grand Rapids, MI: Eerdmans, 2000], 27).

15. "Since the rule of Augustus (died 14 CE), 'father' identified the emperor as Jupiter's agent and the embodiment of Jupiter's rule. He was called *pater patriae*, 'Father of the Fatherland' or 'Father of the Country' (e.g., *Acts of Augustus* 35; Suetonius, *Vespasian* 12). This title not only combined religion and politics, but it also depicted the empire as a large household over which the emperor, like a household's father, exercised authority and protection in return for obedience and submissive devotion" (Warren Carter, *The Roman Empire and the New Testament: An Essential Guide* [Nashville, TN: Abingdon, 2006], 32).

16. Tiberius was referred to as "a good shepherd" (Suetonius, *Tib.* 32). Kings and emperors were generally referred to as "a shepherd of his people" (Dio Chrysostom, *1 Regn.* 13) and "shepherd of peoples" who was to "protect flocks" (Dio Chrysostom, *1 Regn.* 43–44). See Warren Carter, "Matthew and Empire," in *Empire in the New Testament*, ed. Stanley E. Porter and Cynthia Long Westfall (Eugene, OR: Pickwick, 2011), 104–5.

17. Inscribed on a statue of Caesar Claudius; see Winter, *Divine Honours*, 71–72.

18. 1 Tim. 4:10 (NASB).

19. *Tituli Asiae Minoris* 2.760; *IGRR* 4, 584; *P. Oxy.* 1021, lines 2–3; see Winter, *Divine Honours*, 72.

20. See 1 Tim. 3:16 (ESV).

21. Polytheistic pagans referred to Caesar as "god" and "son of god," but Christians used the definite article: Christ is "*the* Son of God." Bruce Winter points out that "this claim put the early Christians on an inevitable ideological clash with their compatriots whose polytheistic view of the divinity could readily incorporate the concept of

the reigning emperor as 'a god, a son of a god,' with men who became gods and some of whom were posthumously awarded perpetual divinity" (*Divine Honours*, 71).

22. See, e.g., Josephus, *War* 4.618.

23. See Winter, *Divine Honours*, 28–43, for a through discussion and translation of this calendar inscription. (Emphasis mine.)

24. Priene, Apamea, Eumeneia, Maeonia, and Dorylaion.

25. See Matthew W. Bates, *Salvation by Allegiance Alone: Rethinking Faith, Works, and the Gospel of Jesus the King* (Grand Rapids, MI: Baker Academic, 2017).

26. Patrick Schreiner mentions "subversion and submission" throughout his important book *Political Gospel: Public Witness in a Politically Crazy World* (Nashville, TN: B&H, 2022). I do wonder if we could take Schreiner's idea one step further. Instead of subversion and submission existing in tension like two sides of the same coin, what if it's more accurate to speak of subversion *through submission*? Here the two concepts are not opposites, nor do they exist in tension. Rather, in God's upside-down kingdom, submitting to the state is a way we subvert the authoritative power of the state, similar to the way Christ defeated the dragon by submitting to the cross.

27. See Gordon D. Fee, *Paul's Letter to the Philippians* (Grand Rapids, MI: Eerdmans, 1995), 25–26.

28. Joseph H. Hellerman, *Embracing Shared Ministry: Power and Status in the Early Church and Why It Matters Today* (Grand Rapids, MI: Kregel, 2013), 85.

29. Hellerman, *Embracing Shared Ministry*, 108.

30. See Hellerman, *Embracing Shared Ministry*, 95, 113. Compared to about 10 percent of the population living under Roman rule

as a whole (see James S. Jeffers, *The Greco-Roman World of the New Testament Era: Exploring the Background of Early Christianity* [Downers Grove, IL: InterVarsity, 1999], 197). Hellerman also says: "It has been recently estimated that about one third of those who belonged to the church at Philippi possessed Roman citizenship" (*Embracing Shared Ministry*, 95).

31. Clement, in Matthew Forrest Lowe, "'This Was Not an Ordinary Death': Empire and Atonement in the Minor Pauline Epistles," in *Empire in the New Testament*, ed. Stanley E. Porter and Cynthia Long Westfall (Eugene, OR: Pickwick, 2011), 208.

32. See Winter, *Divine Honours*, 71–72.

33. See Winter, *Divine Honours*, 250.

34. One of the more interesting suggestions is that "Paul and Silas were accused of being known Jewish revolutionaries opposed to Roman rule and undermining the *pax romana*" (Winter, *Divine Honours*, 251). In response to revolutionary activity in Alexandria, the emperor Claudius had earlier made a decree that it was illegal to "invite in as allies or approve of Jews" suspected of being revolutionaries and "fomenters of what is a general plague infesting the whole world" (*P. Lond.* 1912, lines 96–99, cited in Winter, *Divine Honours*, 251). This parallels the accusation that "Jason has welcomed them into his house. They are all defying Caesar's [that is, Claudius's] decrees" (Acts 17:7). In Thessalonica, Jason and others had harbored Paul and Silas, who, given their message about King Jesus, could easily have been suspected of starting a revolution and therefore being guilty of treason (see Winter, *Divine Honours*, 252).

35. See Lowe, "'This Was Not an Ordinary Death,'" 215–16.

36. Lowe, "'This Was Not an Ordinary Death,'" 216 (emphasis mine).

Chapter 7: This Empire Is Not Our Home

1. The old hymn "This World Is Not My Home" begins with "This world is not my home; I'm just a-passing through. My treasures are laid up somewhere beyond the blue."

2. E.g., Rom. 8:19–23; 1 Cor. 15:20–58. God called creation "good" seven times in Genesis 1–2.

3. The sections that address slaves (2:18–25) and wives (3:1–7) raise many questions, and they certainly feel like a far cry from full liberation. But the fact that Peter addressed slaves and wives directly "would be seen as usurping the prerogative of the head of the household," and it "implied that slaves and women had moral responsibility and choice that was unparalleled in the dominant culture and so was a way of resistance because it seized the initiative from the powerful" (Cynthia Long Westfall, "Running the Gamut: The Varied Responses to Empire in Jewish Christianity," in *Empire in the New Testament*, ed. Stanley E. Porter and Cynthia Long Westfall [Eugene, OR: Pickwick, 2011], 241; cf. Karen H. Jobes, *1 Peter*, 2nd ed. [Grand Rapids, MI: Baker Academic, 2022], 206). Moreover, Peter's instructions to slaves mirror the posture of Christ, which is remarkable. In essence, slaves were to behave like the King of creation, and therefore, in God's kingdom, they were more honorable than the Roman emperor, who was subservient to Christ. "Peter reversed the shame of the slave. A slave no longer had to submit because of social inferiority and degradation—he or she was called to walk in the footsteps of Jesus and be a model of Christ-like behavior to the whole suffering community. This redefinition of the slave's identity struck at the heart of the patronage system and the value of honor in the Roman Empire" (Westfall, "Running the Gamut," 242).

4. Westfall, "Running the Gamut," 240.

5. Westfall, "Running the Gamut," 240.

6. "The theme of exile, announced in the first verse, serves as an introduction to the larger section 1:3—2:10, and with the addition of *paroikoi* in 2:11, continues to underlie the discussion of 2:11—4:11" (Paul J. Achtemeier, *1 Peter: A Commentary on First Peter*, ed. Eldon Jay Epp [Minneapolis: Fortress, 1996], 80).

7. See Achtemeier, *1 Peter*, 81. "In the LXX it occurs only in Gen 23:4; Ps 38:13; in the NT in 1 Pet 1:1; 2:11; Heb 11:13" (Achtemeier, *1 Peter*, 81n33).

8. "Used of Christians," writes Paul Achtemeier, "it describes the fact that because of their unwillingness to adopt the mores of their surrounding society, they can expect the disdainful treatment often accorded exiles (e.g., 1 Pet 4:3–4)" (*1 Peter*, 82).

9. See Achtemeier, *1 Peter*, 82. "The word … appears in the LXX twelve times, in the NT twice (John 7:35; Jas 1:1)" (Achtemeier, *1 Peter*, 82n43).

10. The term *paroikia* can be translated as "foreigner," "sojourn," or "exile." It refers to Israel's time in Egypt in Psalm 105:12; Wisdom 19:10; and Acts 13:17, and to exile in foreign lands in 3 Maccabees 7:19 and Baruch 4:10, 14, 24; see Thomas R. Schreiner, *1, 2 Peter, Jude* (Nashville, TN: B&H, 2003), 82.

11. See Moses Chin, "A Heavenly Home for the Homeless: Aliens and Strangers in 1 Peter," *Tyndale Bulletin* 42, no. 1 (1991): 96–112. Chin, however, emphasizes a cosmological contrast in the two terms—Christians are aliens on earth because they belong in heaven. Other scholars like John Elliott show that Peter had in mind more of a sociological contrast—Christians have been alienated from social norms in light of their conversion to Christ (see John H. Elliott, *1 Peter: A New Translation with Introduction and Commentary* [New York: Doubleday, 2000], 476–83; cf. John H. Elliott, *A Home for the Homeless: A Social-Scientific Criticism of 1 Peter, Its Situation and*

Strategy [Eugene, OR: Wipf and Stock, 2005], 21–49). While the two terms can emphasize something like the transitory nature of life on earth (as in Ps. 119:19 and 1 Chron. 29:15), their predominant use in the LXX and New Testament is much more sociopolitical, and this seems to be what Peter intended here (as opposed to Christians being aliens and strangers on earth because they really belong in heaven).

12. E.g., Acts 7:6, 29; 13:17. See Achtemeier, *1 Peter*, 173–74.

13. That is, the Septuagint (LXX)—the Greek translation of the Hebrew Old Testament.

14. See J. Ramsey Michaels, *1 Peter* (Grand Rapids, MI: Zondervan, 1988), 8, for all these early-church references and several others. (Emphasis mine.)

15. Michaels, *1 Peter*, 8 (emphasis mine).

16. Achtemeier, *1 Peter*, 173.

17. The use of *paroikos* ("sojourner") "can be found from the patriarchal period of Genesis through the monarchic period to that of the exilic, and even that of the inter-testamental.... In other words, the concept of the Israelite nation as one on a *paroikia* ['sojourn'] is something which the Jews were never able to shed, and it may be further argued that it was one of the dominant if not distinguishing marks of the Israelite people" (Chin, "Heavenly Home," 100–101).

18. This view is held by the majority of commentators (see the discussion in Achtemeier, *1 Peter*, 353–54).

19. Martin Luther King Jr., "Letter from Birmingham Jail," April 16, 1963, in *Why We Can't Wait* (Boston: Beacon, 2010), 93. For civil disobedience in Scripture, see Ex. 1:17; Dan. 3:13–18; 6:10–13; Acts 4:18–20; 5:27–29; Heb. 11:23.

20. For *ktisis*, see Mark 16:15; Rom. 1:25; Col. 1:23; cf. Judith 16:14; Tobit 8:5, 15.

21. See DASH Network, accessed July 20, 2023, www.dashnetwork.net.

22. John Garland, quoted in Patton Dodd, "A Texas Congregation Caring for Immigrants Gains a New Understanding of Christianity as a 'Trauma-Healing Movement,'" Faith & Leadership, January 21, 2020, https://faithandleadership.com/texas-congregation-caring -immigrants-gains-new-understanding-christianity-trauma-healing -movement.

23. John Garland, "Asylum Seekers, Undocumented Immigrants, and the Gospel: Dr. Rebecca Poe Hays and John Garland," interview by Preston Sprinkle, *Theology in the Raw*, podcast, episode 895, August 23, 2021, https://theologyintheraw.com/podcast/895-asylum-seekers -undocumented-immigrants-and-the-gospel-dr-rebecca-poe-hays-and -john-garland.

24. Stanley Hauerwas and William H. Willimon, *Resident Aliens: Life in the Christian Colony*, rev. ed. (Nashville, TN: Abingdon, 2014), 41.

Chapter 8: The Apocalypse of Empire

1. "Revelation is the New Testament document that is most critical of the empire.... The confrontation between Christianity and Rome is finally 'gloves off'" (Cynthia Long Westfall, "Running the Gamut: The Varied Responses to Empire in Jewish Christianity," in *Empire in the New Testament*, ed. Stanley E. Porter and Cynthia Long Westfall [Eugene, OR: Pickwick, 2011], 251).

2. Westfall, "Running the Gamut," 253.

3. See Dan. 7–12; 1 Enoch 91:11–17; 93:1–10; 4 Ezra; 2 Baruch.

4. Richard Bauckham, *The Theology of the Book of Revelation* (Cambridge: Cambridge University Press, 1993), 38.

5. See 1 Pet. 5:13; 2 Baruch 67:7; 4 Ezra 15:43–48; Sib. Or. 5.143, 155–61.

6. Greg Carey says that the "seven heads serve a double function, pointing at once to both Rome's famous 'seven hills' and to seven emperors (17:9)" ("The Book of Revelation as Counter-Imperial Script," in *In the Shadow of Empire: Reclaiming the Bible as a History of Faithful Resistance*, ed. Richard A. Horsley [Louisville, KY: Westminster John Knox, 2008], 165).

7. "Who could miss the reference to the whore of Babylon sitting on seven hills (Rev 17:9)?" (Westfall, "Running the Gamut," 254). Cf. David E. Aune: "[It] would be instantly recognizable as a metaphor for Rome" (*Revelation 17–22* [Grand Rapids, MI: Zondervan, 1998], 944).

8. Bauckham, *Theology of the Book of Revelation*, 35–36.

9. Carey, "Book of Revelation as Counter-Imperial Script," 166. "Most interpreters ... would identify the first beast, from the sea ... as the Roman Empire, the emperor ... or imperial power. The second beast, from the earth ... is then seen as those who promote the imperial cult, perhaps local government and/or religious officials in and around cities like Ephesus and Pergamum" (Michael J. Gorman, *Reading Revelation Responsibly: Uncivil Worship and Witness; Following the Lamb into the New Creation* [Eugene, OR: Cascade Books, 2011], 124). Bauckham says the second beast "probably represents the imperial priesthood in the cities of the province of Asia" and connects it to "the false prophet" in Revelation 16:13; 19:20 (*Theology of the Book of Revelation*, 38).

10. Carey, "Book of Revelation as Counter-Imperial Script," 165.

11. Gorman, *Reading Revelation Responsibly*, 33.

12. Westfall, "Running the Gamut," 255.

13. Gorman, *Reading Revelation Responsibly*, 125.

14. Bauckham, *Theology of the Book of Revelation*, 156. See too M. Eugene Boring's apt comment: "The beast is not merely 'Rome'.... It is the inhuman, anti-human arrogance of empire which has come to expression in Rome—but not only there.... All who support and promote the cultural religion, in or out of the church, however Lamb-like they may appear, are agents of the beast. All propaganda that entices humanity to idolize human empire is an expression of this beastly power that wants to appear Lamb-like" (*Revelation* [Louisville, KY: John Knox, 1989], 156–57).

15. See Rom. 8:37–39; Eph. 1:20–21; 2:2; 3:10; 6:12; Col. 1:16; 2:10, 15; cf. 1 Cor. 2:8.

16. Markus Barth, *Ephesians: Introduction, Translation, and Commentary on Chapters 1–3* (Garden City, NY: Doubleday, 1974), 175. Paul was clearly referring to demonic forces of evil (see especially Eph. 6:12). But he was drawing on the typical Jewish view that saw these spiritual forces as working together with earthly governing rulers. "In Judaism," writes New Testament scholar Andrew Lincoln, "there was the belief that God had delegated authority over the nations to angelic beings. The notion that what happens among these beings in heaven affects what happens among the nations on earth is reflected in Dan 10:13, 20" (*Ephesians* [Grand Rapids, MI: Zondervan, 1990], 63; see, e.g., 2 Enoch 20–22). Lincoln argues, however, that in Ephesians Paul was primarily thinking of spiritual powers and not governing authorities, while Walter Wink argues that both are in view (see *Naming the Powers: The Language of Power in the New Testament* [Philadelphia: Fortress, 1984]).

17. For an international perspective on Revelation and empire, see David Rhoads, ed., *From Every People and Nation: The Book of Revelation in Intercultural Perspective* (Minneapolis: Fortress, 2005).

18. Bauckham, *Theology of the Book of Revelation*, 74.

19. Bauckham, *Theology of the Book of Revelation*, 64 (emphasis mine).

20. Gorman, *Reading Revelation Responsibly*, 111.

21. The kind of persecution in Revelation was somewhat different from what some Christians experience today when they preach Jesus in countries where Christianity is illegal.

22. See Gorman, *Reading Revelation Responsibly*, 93, for a description and a picture of the ancient ruins.

23. Carey, "Book of Revelation as Counter-Imperial Script," 163.

24. Carey, "Book of Revelation as Counter-Imperial Script," 172.

25. See Isa. 13:1–22; 21:1–10; Jer. 25:12–38; Jer. 50–51; Ezek. 26–28.

26. Richard Bauckham, *The Bible in Politics: How to Read the Bible Politically*, 2nd ed. (London: SPCK, 2010), 92.

27. Bauckham, *Bible in Politics*, 93.

28. Bauckham, *Bible in Politics*, 93.

29. Nilay Saiya, *The Global Politics of Jesus: A Christian Case for Church-State Separation* (New York: Oxford University Press, 2022), 244.

Chapter 9: Exile as Prophetic Witness

1. Daniel L. Smith-Christopher, *The Religion of the Landless: The Social Context of the Babylonian Exile* (Eugene, OR: Wipf and Stock, 2015), 214.

2. See, for instance, Amy E. Black, ed., *Five Views on the Church and Politics* (Grand Rapids, MI: Zondervan, 2015).

3. These three approaches often go by various names. For instance, some call the Detachment view "Isolation." I'm not as concerned about the specific terms used to describe these approaches as I am the content of each. In terms of the content, I'm indebted to Nilay Saiya's fine summary in his excellent book *The Global Politics of Jesus: A Christian Case for Church-State Separation* (New York: Oxford University Press, 2022), 38–83.

4. E.g., Isa. 3:14; 5:8; Amos 5:11, 21–24; 8:5; Mic. 3:3, 9–10.

5. Saiya, *Global Politics of Jesus*, 44. The Transformation view is similar to what Stanley Hauerwas and William Willimon describe as an "*activist* church," which is often "more concerned with the building of a better society than with the reformation of the church" (*Resident Aliens: Life in the Christian Colony*, rev. ed. [Nashville, TN: Abingdon, 2014], 44–45).

6. Saiya, *Global Politics of Jesus*, 46.

7. Martin Luther King Jr. (speech, UCLA, Los Angeles, CA, April 27, 1965), https://newsroom.ucla.edu/stories/archivist-finds-long-lost -recording-of-martin-luther-king-jr-s-speech-at-ucla.

8. "When the church does interact with the state, it takes the form of ad hoc, discriminating engagement in which the church makes no effort to cultivate a relationship of privilege with the powers" (Saiya, *Global Politics of Jesus*, 65).

9. Saiya, *Global Politics of Jesus*, 49.

10. One simply needs to stroll down the national mall in Washington, DC, from the temple that houses Abraham Lincoln, past all the monuments and shrines, to the Capitol Building, where one can stand in the Rotunda and look up to see a majestic painting of George

Washington being deified in the exact same way the Roman Caesars were depicted. For a very fair analysis of America and the Roman Empire, see Peter J. Leithart, *Between Babel and Beast: America and Empires in Biblical Perspective* (Eugene, OR: Cascade Books, 2012).

11. See John H. Yoder, "See How They Go with Their Face to the Sun," in John H. Yoder, *For the Nations: Essays Evangelical and Public* (Grand Rapids, MI: Eerdmans, 1997), 77.

12. This is not to discount the many ways in which the church has had a positive effect on the empire or on sociopolitical structures as a whole. As James K. A. Smith and others have pointed out, there are many "creators of the gospel" that have made their imprint on liberal democracies around the world (see James K. A. Smith, *Awaiting the King: Reforming Public Theology*, Cultural Liturgies, vol. 3 [Grand Rapids, MI: Baker Academic, 2017], especially 91–130). To my mind, Smith's political theology is the best, most nuanced version of what may be considered a Transformation viewpoint. While I appreciate his emphasis on "ad hoc collaboration" (see pp. 216–21) rather than partisan allegiance, I still find his theology of empire underdeveloped.

13. Saiya, *Global Politics of Jesus*, 74.

14. Saiya, *Global Politics of Jesus*, 77.

15. See Saiya, *Global Politics of Jesus*, 71–82, 86–126.

16. Saiya, *Global Politics of Jesus*, 63.

17. Saiya, *Global Politics of Jesus*, 70.

18. Saiya, *Global Politics of Jesus*, 65. See also Lee C. Camp, *Scandalous Witness: A Little Political Manifesto for Christians* (Grand Rapids, MI: Eerdmans, 2020), 164–72.

19. Hauerwas and Willimon, *Resident Aliens*, 38, 41.

20. Hauerwas and Willimon, *Resident Aliens*, 46.

21. Far from separating ourselves from societal efforts to pursue justice, the "church can participate in secular movements against war, against hunger, and against other forms of inhumanity, but it sees this as part of its necessary proclamatory action." In other words, it "knows that its most credible form of witness (and the most 'effective' thing it can do for the world) is the actual creation of a living, breathing, visible community of faith" (Hauerwas and Willimon, *Resident Aliens*, 47).

22. See John Gramlich, "What the Data Says about Gun Deaths in the U.S.," Pew Research Center, April 26, 2023, www.pewresearch.org/short-reads/2023/04/26/what-the-data-says-about-gun-deaths-in-the-u-s.

23. "Together Chicago Overview Video," YouTube video, 3:46, June 21, 2022, https://youtu.be/C9cKViAB9WA.

24. "Together Chicago Overview Video."

25. For this section, see my book *Nonviolence: The Revolutionary Way of Jesus* (Colorado Springs: David C Cook, 2021), 166–70.

26. Paul does go on to command Christians to "do what is right" (13:3) and "be afraid" (13:4), but these are both extensions of submitting to governing authorities.

27. See Gen. 37–50; Dan. 1–6; Est. 1–10.

28. Debra Reid points out, "Esther herself is not flawless in the story: hiding her identity contradicts Jewish law; the process of becoming Xerxes' queen is unsavoury; instituting laws that are vicious appears morally indefensible. But God works with these human responses as his sovereign will for his people emerges" (*Esther: An Introduction and Commentary* [Downers Grove, IL: IVP Academic, 2008], 52). Other scholars argue that, as a young woman of that time, Esther lacked any agency to resist the evil she was dragged into. For a brief discussion of these issues, see Barry G. Webb, *Five Festal Garments: Christian*

Reflections on the Song of Songs, Ruth, Lamentations, Ecclesiastes and Esther (Downers Grove, IL: IVP Academic, 2000), 118–21.

Chapter 10: Living as Exiles in Babylon

1. Stanley Hauerwas, *The Peaceable Kingdom: A Primer in Christian Ethics* (Notre Dame, IN: University of Notre Dame Press, 1991), 100 (emphasis mine).

2. David French, "The Pro-life Movement's Work Is Just Beginning," *Atlantic*, June 24, 2022, www.theatlantic.com/ideas/archive/2022/06 /pro-life-dobbs-roe-culture-of-life/661394.

3. See Aaron Earls, "7 in 10 Women Who Have Had an Abortion Identify as a Christian," Lifeway Research, December 3, 2021, https://research.lifeway.com/2021/12/03/7-in-10-women-who-have -had-an-abortion-identify-as-a-christian.

4. Earls, "7 in 10 Women."

5. Earls, "7 in 10 Women."

6. For a Christian perspective on the news, see Jeffrey Bilbro, *Reading the Times: A Literary and Theological Inquiry into the News* (Downers Grove, IL: IVP Academic, 2021).

7. Even nonreligious people like Matt Taibbi recognize this; see *Hate Inc.: Why Today's Media Makes Us Despise One Another* (New York: OR Books, 2021).

8. One healthy way to stay informed is by following nonpartisan out-lets like *The Pour Over* (podcast and newsletter) that focus on simply keeping people informed while reminding them that Christ is king.

9. See Preston Sprinkle, *Nonviolence: The Revolutionary Way of Jesus* (Colorado Springs: David C Cook, 2021), 202.

"This book is my fragile attempt to help us think more deeply and love more widely through a topic that sometimes lacks both."

—Preston Sprinkle

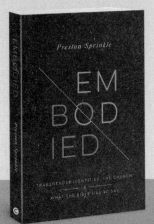

An Invitation for Christians to Join the Transgender Conversation

With careful research and an engaging style, Sprinkle explores:

- What it means to be transgender, non-binary, gender-queer, and how these identies relate to being male and female

- Why most stereotypes about what it means to be a man and woman come from culture and not the Bible

- What the Bible says about humans created in God's image as male and female and how this relates to transgender experiences

- Moral questions surrounding medical interventions such as sex reassignment surgery

- Which pronouns to use and how to navigate the bathroom debate

Available in print, digital, and audio
wherever books are sold

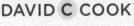

DAVID **C** COOK

transforming lives together

AN INVITATION TO EMBODY TRUTH AND GRACE

Biblical scholar Preston Sprinkle offers a thoughtful and gracious treatment of one of the most divisive topics of our time—whether the Bible supports same-sex marriage.

This highly relevant exploration of the top 21 arguments in favor of same-sex marriage equips us with biblical guidance, historical background, and a gracious posture for having meaningful conversations about contentious issues. In *Does the Bible Support Same-Sex Marriage?*, biblical scholar Preston Sprinkle explores what the Bible really says about one of today's most controversial subjects, equipping parents, church leaders, and friends to communicate truth with love.

Available in print, digital, and audio
wherever books are sold